DIVINE FOOD

Israeli and Palestinian
Food Culture and Recipes

gestalten

CONTENTS

Cover Image: **Za'atar pastry,
a dish typical of the cuisine of
northern Israel** (see page 54).

INTRODUCTION
4   Food from the promised Land

THE NORTH
12   About the Region

RECIPES FROM THE SOUTH
238 Flavors of the Desert

THE BASICS
282 Spices, Stocks, and
      Building Block

RECIPES FROM THE NORTH

JERUSALEM

RECIPES FROM TEL AVIV

TEL AVIV

RECIPES FROM JERUSALEM

THE SOUTH

FOOD FROM THE PROMISED LAND

From large cities with diverse populations to tiny villages built into the hillsides, everyone can unite over food. Opposite page: **Modern, bustling, beautifully designed spaces, such as Ha'achim restaurant in Tel Aviv, signal to diners that they're about to experience a new take on Israeli cuisine.**

From regional to global, ancient to contemporary, many a dish in this part of the world dates back millennia, has a story that could fill a history book, and has been recreated in a hundred new ways. With flavors that echo across the ages and also stir up plenty of debate, this is food with roots and wings.

The argument started with an eggplant. Roasted whole over a charcoal grill. Peeled carefully. Drizzled with olive oil. Served with tahini. So simple, and so delicious. But an eggplant is never just an eggplant—not in Israel, where even the simplest dish can stir up a heated debate. Newspaper headlines relayed the play-by-play as leading chefs, both Jews and Arabs, traded barbs over who had invented the recipe. It seemed like everyone loved it—but who could rightfully lay claim to it? That simple dish had somehow become symbolic of the battle over new Israeli cuisine.

Just as everyone can lay claim to this region, with its countless cultural shifts, border drawings and redrawings, destruction, rebirth, and growth over the last century, everyone can lay claim to its food. A simple meal can represent a wide spectrum of personal histories, stem from a number of sources, and carry a considerable amount of cultural, historical, and political weight in every bite. So it is with staples like hummus and falafel, and so it was with this simple, baladi (local variety) eggplant.

The story of the great eggplant debate illustrates some of what makes the cuisine of this region so special. Just consider: The inspiration for the dish comes from baba ghanoush, a Middle Eastern dish of roasted eggplant flesh mixed with tahini. But where did baba ghanoush come from, and who was responsible for adding it to the modern Israeli menu? Baba ghanoush is an inseparable part of the mezze spread of what was once called Greater Syria (modern-day Syria, Lebanon, Jordan, Israel, and the Palestinian Territories.) It appears frequently on the traditional menu of Palestinian Arabs living in Israel, as well as that of Jews who immigrated to Israel from Arab countries.

Some claim its roots lie in Turkish cuisine. For four centuries, Greater Syria and the Land of Israel within it was part of the Ottoman Empire. Jews from Turkey and the Balkans brought similar dishes with them to Israel; and long before that, Jews expelled from Spain in 1492 found a new home in the Ottoman Empire, perhaps bringing their love for the eggplant along with them. If we are going to bother to go that far back, though, we might as well acknowledge the eggplant's origins in India. The tahini on top is made from African-grown sesame these days, since Israel is no longer the center of sesame farming and processing it once was. Greater Syria, Turkey, India, Africa—can this dish really be labeled "local" anymore?

But the point, of course, was not where the ingredients were sourced, but where the true spirit of the dish lay. By claiming it as their own, Israeli chefs were attempting to add a layer of their own mythology to the dish's creation story. Meanwhile, Palestinian chefs were simply trying to take back what they saw as rightfully theirs. For each side, claiming the dish would mean grasping something central and critical to the understanding of Israel, somehow crystallizing its own creation myth and clarifying the various transformations it had undergone to arrive at the modern table. All this in a bite of something delicious that hundreds and perhaps thousands of people enjoy in Israel every day. A bite that all those people shared, regardless of their

Opposite page: **In this part of the world, meals can be boisterous affairs. Most dishes are made to be shared, and a meal is as much about the cooking as it is about getting together with family and friends.** Above: **These stuffed Arabic pancakes, called Ataif, are usually served at the end of the meal, along with Turkish coffee.**

A simple meal can represent a wide spectrum of personal histories and carry a considerable amount of cultural, historical, and political weight in every bite.

Above: **Tel Aviv street life turns to night-life as the sun goes down and restaurants keep outdoor table service going.** Below and opposite page: **Grilled whole fish and cauliflower and chickpeas with tahini are two perennial favorites.**

backgrounds, whether they realized it or not. It is that last thought that matters most—good food has the power to bring us all together. In the kitchen. At the dinner table. At the market. In the neighborhood café or the fine restaurant. While modern-day Israel is less than 70 years old—hardly enough time to develop a deep-rooted culinary tradition—the cultural-geographical region itself boasts a rich and complex culinary history stretching back millennia. Waves of conquerors, merchants, and pilgrims visiting the Holy Land over centuries left their traces, and one can still identify remnants of Greek, Roman, Byzantine, Mamluk, Crusader, and Ottoman influences in the local culture. Meanwhile, Jews the world over had lived for thousands of years in many different places, adopting and adapting the cuisines of their surrounding cultures. That meant immigrants from various countries had little in common, apart from the laws governing kosher food, and a small number of dishes served on the Sabbath and Jewish holidays. With the establishment of the state of Israel, the time was ripe for a new Israeli cuisine. A cuisine that drew from all of the influences available. In the first few years of the country's existence, years of austerity when little meat was available, Arab dishes like hummus with tahini and falafel were adopted by Jews, turning them into "national" Israeli dishes, much to the dissatisfaction of the Palestinians, who saw this cultural appropriation as a mirror of the occupation, a symbol of the continuing Arab-Israeli conflict. For many years, local Arab restaurants were referred to in Hebrew as "Oriental," a vague term that avoided engaging in a definition of Palestinian identity through its cuisine. A true culinary discourse only began to evolve in the 1960s and 1970s, when the country's economy had begun to stabilize, and a unique Israeli fusion cuisine took its first steps. Various ethnic dishes—North African couscous and shakshuka, European chopped liver and schnitzel, the Turkish-Balkan burek, and Yemenite dough pastries—began to mingle on the streets and in the home kitchen.

In the 1980s, security and economic stability led to a growing interest in leisure culture, and through it, cuisine. Third-generation immigrants, no longer burdened by the same diaspora complexes that characterized their predecessors, rediscovered the rich ethnic cuisines their grandparents had left behind in the old country. Despite the complex political situation, the worldwide trend of searching for local, quality raw ingredients encouraged new interest in traditional Palestinian dishes, which soon became one of the most prominent sources of inspiration for new Israeli cuisine.

The lack of clear-cut traditions still pushes local and international chefs to innovate, and the influence of Palestinian cuisine has only grown in recent years, its stature now matching and perhaps surpassing the legacy of various immigrant cuisines from Jewish communities around the world. Dishes from Sephardic Jewish communities, which originate in places with geographical conditions similar to those of Israel—North Africa, Iraq, Turkey, and the Balkans—are given preference over dishes from the kitchens of the Ashkenazi Jewish communities of Eastern Europe (though you will find them here as well).

Olive oil, lemon, garlic, cured meat, lamb, tahini, and local herbs and spices stand as major symbols of Israel's burgeoning culinary language. The biblical fruits of the Seven Species—wheat, barley, grapes, olives, figs, dates, and pomegranates—drove a thriving economy in ancient times and still star in modern local menus. Joining them is a selection of Mediterranean fish, seafood, and fresh vegetables grown through traditional farming or sophisticated industrial agriculture. No Israeli meal—breakfast, lunch, or dinner—comes without a selection of colorful vegetables, chopped raw into a salad or served alongside, seared on the grill or lightly steamed. The use of the tabun, the region's traditional clay oven, is becoming more and more widespread. Ingredients are never concealed by dense broths or complex sauces, but rather accentuated with olive oil, Yogurt, smen (salted fermented butter), or tomatoes.

Meanwhile, young Israeli chefs trained in Michelin-starred restaurants in Europe applied modern cooking techniques to traditional recipes upon their return. Young Palestinian chefs also trained in professional kitchens worldwide as they sought new ways of expressing the culinary traditions passed down by their ancestors. All this created a fascinating and thriving local restaurant

This is what matters most—good food has the power to bring us all together. In the kitchen. At the dinner table. At the market.

scene, signaling to the world that the flavors of the Middle East are every bit as complex and laudatory as those of culinary stalwarts like France or Italy. Israel's cuisine never really lost its "fruit-of-the-land" qualities—it just grew up a bit. In spite of its myriad origins and far-reaching past, new Israeli cuisine is still seeking out its direction and language, feeling out new flavors and pathways. Perhaps in response to the heavy historical baggage—or appropriately for the Middle Eastern climate—it is generally a light, Mediterranean cuisine, intuitive and creative, prepared using methods that underscore and highlight the dominant flavors of local ingredients. It is a cuisine still in its infancy, and yet its prospects are multifold, its great expectations made greater by the weight of the many cultures symbolized by and carried within every dish. And it is that cuisine that we will share together in the pages that follow.

Israel sits at the junction of three continents: Asia, Europe, and Africa. Throughout history, it has served as a key intersection of trade routes from China to Spain. Though one of the world's smallest countries (approx. 20,000 km²), Israel enjoys a rare geographical and climatic diversity. Cold weather prevails on the highest peaks in the North, which are covered in snow every winter. The Jordan Valley, stretching down from the Jordan River, is the lowest place on earth, with a warm, eerily calm climate that finds its nadir down by the salt-encrusted banks of the Dead Sea. The coastal regions and the central hills enjoy a comfortable Mediterranean climate, while the southern deserts—the Negev and the Arava—are dry, arid, and otherworldly.

The freedom with which culinary traditions mix in Israel makes it difficult to categorize dishes by their home regions, but distinct areas with geographical, cultural, and culinary singularities are slowly emerging. For the purposes of this book, we have divided the land into four chapters, reflecting four distinct landscapes and the corresponding properties of their local cuisines: the mountainous, rural North, demarcated by the borders between Israel and Lebanon, Syria, and Jordan; Jerusalem, Israel's historic capital, and the mountains around it; Tel Aviv, the Mediterranean shore and the central region; and the cultivated deserts and settlements of the South.

In each chapter we discuss the history, culture, and context of each region. We have done our best to capture the unique spirit of each one by translating the aromas, sounds, and tastes in a vivid and authentic manner. Ultimately, each region—and its cuisine—is a product of its people; the colorful, brash, and bold folk that bring this whole orchestra to life. Every country, every town, and every market has its legends, its kings and princes, its queens and mothers. Without intimately knowing them, you have barely scratched the surface. We have made many friends while making this book. Without them we would have nothing.

We hope this book will bring forth a vision for a better future; one in which we can return to a simplicity and to what really matters:

Life. Food. People.

Israeli and Palestinian chefs sought new ways of expressing the culinary traditions passed down by their ancestors.

Opposite page: **Iris sells spices, nuts, and seeds in Tel Aviv's Levinsky Market.** Below: **Colorful sweets arrayed to catch the customer's eye on the way out.**

THE NORTH

FOUR SEASONS AND FINE FOOD

Bordered by Lebanon, Syria, and the Mediterranean Sea, the North matches its somewhat precarious geographical position with a rich cultural and eco-logical heritage. The only region in Israel with a temperate climate and four distinct seasons, the North takes advantage of high altitudes and varied terrains to produce a rich cornucopia of fruits, vegetables, and spices.

The seaport city of Acre, the tranquil Sea of Galilee, and the stark, rocky Golan Heights reflect a multifaceted, deeply traditional culinary heritage. Cooking and eating practices are built around the changing seasons, and elements of the cuisine of Greater Syria still hold sway.

Many local produce varieties originate in little plots farmed with traditional methods using ancient know-how passed down through generations.

On early summer mornings in Galilee, the open-air markets gradually fill with grape-leaf merchants toting white plastic sacks crammed with fresh green leaves on their backs. Used for stuffing, the grape leaves are stacked in tall mounds around the market.

Traders pile crates of fresh vegetables on their stands: long green pods of lubiya, solid little okra pods, and local (or baladi) varieties of cucumbers and zucchini. Among them are the bottle-shaped kar'a zucchini, with its withered appearance and divine taste; the fakos, or Armenian cucumber, with a pale and slightly hairy exterior; and the harosh, a baby melon picked before it ripens. Never grown on an industrial level, these varieties originate in little plots farmed with traditional methods using ancient know-how passed down through generations. They are just a few examples of the rich ecological heritage of the north, where terrain and altitude vary dramatically—the only

The bulbous kar'a zucchini and the fresh green leaves used to make stuffed grape leaves (opposite page) are sold at markets in Galilee, usually by small local farmers.

Here, in one of the most religiously and ethnically diverse regions of Israel, Muslims, Jews, Christians, Druze, and Circassians live—and eat—side by side.

region of Israel with anything close to a temperate growing climate and four distinct seasons.

Here, in one of the most religiously and ethnically diverse regions of Israel, Muslims, Jews, Christians, Druze, and Circassians—a people from the Northern Caucasus who were expelled from their homeland by Czarist Russia and resettled by the Ottoman Empire—live side by side. Despite ongoing political, religious, and social tensions in Israel, the north still retains the cosmopolitan atmosphere of historic Greater Syria, which includes modern-day Syria, Lebanon, Jordan, Israel, and Palestine.

Before the mid-twentieth century, the region was ruled by several empires. Each left its mark on local traditions. Shami cuisine, the cuisine of Greater Syria, was common to all residents of the geographical and cultural space. The cuisine of Nazareth and Acre still closely mirror that of Beirut and Damascus. This shared culinary heritage is characterized by typical ingredients like olive oil and lamb, traditional techniques such as cooking with yogurt, and similar customs, like the culture of meze—little shared plates of cold and warm dishes served with arak, a popular anise-based alcoholic drink. Most of the wheat consumed today in Israel is imported, but small flour mills in this area still process locally grown wheat into bulgur, semolina, and bread flour. Family-owned bakeries produce a range of typical Middle Eastern flatbreads. They have recently been joined by boutique bakeries offering their own varieties of sourdough breads, informed by French and Californian bread-making culture. But even some weeks before it ripens, the wheat yields its own special treasure. Freekeh—a type of green wheat described in the Bible—is roasted in the open field directly after harvesting and becomes the base of many traditional dishes,

INTRODUCING...
THE SABRA

Called a prickly pear or a cactus pear in the most of the world, the sabra reaches its peak in July and August, when small farm stands line Israeli roads selling to passersby. Their color can range from green to yellow to a flushed golden pink, and their insides are as tender as their outsides are tough. Rumored to have been imported from parts of South America and the Southwest United States over 100 years ago, prickly pears have now become such an integral part of the Israeli landscape, their name has even become a stand-in for a proud, native-born Israeli.

In Galilee, the open-air markets
gradually fill with grape-leaf
merchants toting white plastic sacks
crammed with fresh green leaves.

BEYOND ZA'ATAR: COMMON SPICE BLENDS IN ISRAEL

Although za'atar, the spice blend made of sumac, salt, thyme, and sesame seeds is ubiquitous here, Jewish and Arab chefs have begun to bring in a series of other flavor profiles from around the world: Zhug, a spicy Yemeni paste made with green chilis, cilantro, garlic, lemon, and a mix of cumin, coriander, and cardamom, often used as an accompaniment to hummus. Hawaj, another Yemeni spice blend of ginger, cinnamon, cardamom, and cloves that can be used to add flavor to desserts or savory dishes. Baharat, an Iraqi spice blend used to flavor meaty stews is a combination of black pepper, cardamom, cloves, nutmeg, coriander seed, paprika, and chili.

Deep red sumac berries are harvested by local farmers,
then dried and ground into a powder. Wild herbs,
used for food and folk medicine, are still a key element
in local nutrition.

much like rice and grains elsewhere in the world. Meanwhile, in Haifa, the coastal city laid out on the slopes of Mount Carmel, seafood restaurants offer the day's freshest catch while Israeli and Arab eateries, from the luxurious to the hole-in-the-wall, rub shoulders, offering their own takes on decades- or even centuries-old dishes. Farther up the coast, when the sea begins to cool at summer's end, the fishermen of Acre sail to port each morning with a selection of grouper—the king of local fish—as well as drum, red snapper, blue crabs, and tiger shrimp. Every occasion, religious or secular, becomes a celebration of the fruits of the land. Personal connections between those who grow and sell them, and those who make culinary magic with them are forged to be deep and long-lasting—it is not uncommon for farmers to supply the same restaurants for years.

There are unusual varieties to look out for, many of which only come to market for a short time each year. Some are farmed; others are foraged, like tangy green wild plums, purple and yellow figs, and the orange prickly pear known as the sabra (which has also become a slang term for those born in Israel). From the high peaks of the Galilee and Golan mountains come cherries and wild forest berries, while the mountain slopes are home to grapes harvested for local wineries.

Oil made from local olives, particularly those picked in fall around the venerable village of Rameh, have been renowned since ancient times. Oil presses abound in the region, some still using traditional millstones that were once operated by donkeys. Arab and Jewish farmers can still be seen hurrying in and out of them, carrying crates of just-picked green and black olives that will be made into the delicious golden liquid that graces nearly every local dish.

Above: **Eclectic shops like Marwan Kurdi's in Acre sell local spices, forming a crucial part of the culinary landscape.**
Right: **Everyone has an opinion on where to find the best version of a dish, but some of Israel's tastiest food can be found where the decor is sparse and the company is warm, like at the Abu Elias hummus restaurant in Acre.**

Dishes like this one take advantage
of the sea's freshest catch—combined
with locally grown spices and ancient
cooking techniques, of course.

Family-owned bakeries produce a range of typical Middle Eastern flatbreads.

Left: **Turkish coffee is brewed as it has been for years at Abu Salem's café in Nazareth's old city.** Opposite page: **Locals gather to play cards at the café.**

Cafés are much-loved meeting places for locals—many of whom have been visiting their favorites almost daily for years to sip coffee, play cards, and discuss the day's events.

The most popular olive variety, the suri, a mispronunciation of the name tzurian, originates near Tyre, a small town in southern Lebanon. Its tangy, dominant flavors produce wonderful cured olives.

Sumac is another local delicacy with a sharp, near-citrusy flavor used in cooking since long before the lemon dominated Mediterranean cuisine. Its deep red berries are harvested by local farmers in late fall, then dried and ground to a powder. Wild herbs, used for food and folk medicine, are still a key element of winter nutrition. An unexpected gift, they flourish in uncultivated areas and between village houses, and are harvested by the wives of the fellahin (Arabic for farmers). The aromatic green leaves of za'atar, for example, are used in fresh salads and also dried and combined with roasted sesame, salt, and sumac to create the famed za'atar spice mix. Tender sprigs of wild fennel, with their intoxicating anise fragrance, are an

INTRODUCING...
ATAIF

Dessert's answer to the dumpling, ataif are sweet Arabic pancakes with origins in Levantine cuisine (basically, that of all the regions surrounding Israel). They can be filled with a variety of fruits, nuts, or creams, then served at the end of a meal along with a good strong Turkish coffee. Quite fluffy and yeasty, with characteristic air bubbles and a nice burnish, ataif pockets are made much like western pancakes or crepes: by spooning small amounts of liquid batter into a pan and then flipping them over. Once filled, these soft pastries can then be fried or baked, then drizzled with orange blossom water or rosewater for a final glorious finish.

The fragrant smell of cooking can drift easily in Nazareth's Old Town, where people live practically on top of each other.

The process by which green coffee beans are turned into the rich drink beloved the world over is a complex one. The Fahoums do everything on a small, personal scale and it is easy to taste the difference.

This spread: **The Fahoum Family has been roasting and grinding coffee beans in their roasting house in Nazareth's Old City for many years.**

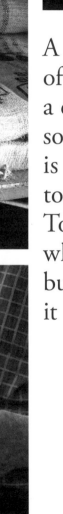

A delicacy, a gift of friendship, or a crucial aid to socializing—coffee is many things to many people. To the Fahoums, who are in the business of coffee, it is a way of life.

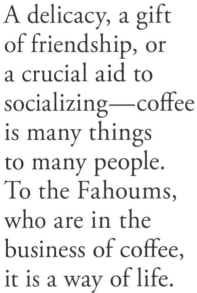

OLIVE OIL—
LIQUID GOLD

If the country's cuisine had one unifying, essential ingredient, it would undoubtedly be olive oil. This precious golden liquid has been extracted for centuries, its color and flavor notes as complex as wine—and just as reflective of terroir. Olive oil can be used as a garnish, a base for a salad dressing, a preserving method, or the first step in a complex sauce or stew. Its color can range from gold to green, with a floral, earthy, acidic, or even metallic flavor. One thing is certain, however: if it has no flavor, it is probably not pure olive oil, so look for bottles from trusted growers and always taste before you buy.

Oil made from local olives has been renowned since ancient times. Oil presses abound in the region, and the delicious golden liquid graces nearly every local dish.

essential ingredient in egg and lentil dishes, as well as a natural, breath-freshening chewing gum. Cyclamen and ox-tongue leaves are used in rice and meat dishes. Green stalks of mallow, chicory, asparagus, and wild spinach are collected in bundles, and even the simplest of wild-herb recipes inevitably begins with a pan full of olive oil and onions. The ideals of hard work and sacrifice, and the creed of living off the land have deep roots here. This becomes most obvious in spring, when the land's growth and renewal yields three major components of regional cuisine: lamb (local lamb meat has an intense, dominant flavor and is frequently grilled in an assortment of recipes), fresh dairy products like yogurt and labaneh from sheep's milk, and wheat.

When it comes to the cuisine of northern Israel, it is a good bet that the ingredients will be as fresh as possible—plucked from land or sea or farm just that morning—and that every recipe, no matter how simple, will have many homes, multiple versions, and a history that could probably fill its very own book.

Moshe Lev Sercarz, a farmer and olive oil manufacturer from Upper Galilee, sorts through his olives personally to find the best ones to transform into his aromatic olive oil.

Street scenes from Nazareth and Acre, where the clock tower watches over work, play, and cooking at all times of day.

Hummus with Pine	חומוס עם צנובר	25
Hummus With foul	חומוס עם פול	20
Hummus with meat	חומוס עם בשר	35
Hummus	חומוס	20
Foul	פול	20
Moshawash	מסבחה	20
Tahina	טחינה	20
Labanie	לבנה	20
Omlet+Chips + Hummus	חביתה + חומוס	25
Chips	צ'יפס	15
Falafel Salad Hummus	פלאפל+סלט	25

When it comes to the cuisine of northern Israel, it is a good bet that the ingredients will be as fresh as possible— plucked from land or sea or farm just that morning.

GIFTS FROM LAND AND SEA

Recipes from the North include pastries and flatbreads, soups and roasts, fresh salads and bright vegetable dishes, as well as a few local takes on that staple of world cuisine, the dumpling. Perhaps you will be surprised by just how many of these dishes feel familiar, but you will also be intrigued by some flavor combinations you may never have tasted before.

Baked eggs (page 48)
from the kitchen of
Fauzi Azar Inn, Nazareth.

ARUGULA SALAD WITH FIGS AND SABRAS

This typical Israeli summer salad contrasts the bitterness of arugula leaves with the sweetness of ripe figs and sabras, two ingredients with special significance in the region. The fig is one of the Biblical Seven Species (page 297), while the sabra (page 17), also known as the prickly pear or cactus pear, has become a slang term for an Israeli-born Jew.

INGREDIENTS

1 green hot chili (Anaheim pepper or any mild variety)
1 tomato, crushed
1 garlic clove, minced
1 tbsp. parsley
3 tbsp. olive oil
1¼ lb. (500 g) arugula
6 ripe fresh figs, quartered
3 sabras (prickly pears), peeled and sliced
1 tbsp. black olives, pitted

DIRECTIONS

With tongs, hold the chili over an open flame until its skin is completely charred. Transfer to a cutting board and use a chef's knife to carefully remove the skin, seeds, and membranes.
Chop the chili as finely as possible and place in a small bowl.
Add the crushed tomato, garlic, parsley and olive oil to the chili.
Mix well and season with salt and pepper.
Combine arugula, figs, sabras, and olives in a serving bowl and distribute dressing evenly.

GOOD TO KNOW

If you do not have a gas stove, slice the chili in half, put both halves face down on a baking sheet, and set your oven to broil. Remove the chili when the skin is completely charred.

ACRE-STYLE VEGETABLE SALAD

Chopped vegetable salads are a celebration of the land's bounty, served with almost every meal. Every region has its own version: Acre's, for instance, includes hot peppers and cubes of fresh lemons. In order to get the most out of this salad's flavors, all ingredients must be high quality and extremely fresh, and chopping must be fine and precise.

INGREDIENTS

4 Lebanese cucumbers
3 ripe tomatoes
1 small onion
1 lemon
1 romaine lettuce heart
1 clove garlic, minced
1 tsp. finely chopped fresh green
   chili (Anaheim pepper or
   any mild variety), deseeded
1 tbsp. finely chopped
   mint leaves
½ cup (15 g) finely chopped
   parsley
3 tbsp. extra virgin olive oil
Juice of 1 lemon
1 pinch salt
1 pinch freshly ground
   black pepper

DIRECTIONS

Dice cucumbers, tomatoes, and onion so that all are approximately the same size.
Peel lemon and cut into sections, discarding the white membrane before dicing.
Cut lettuce heart into thin strips.
Combine cucumbers, tomatoes, onion, lemon, and lettuce in a large salad bowl with the rest of the ingredients.

FREEKEH AND ASPARAGUS SALAD

Freekeh is green roasted wheat with a wonderfully smoky taste, harvested in spring by local fellahin before the wheat plant ripens, and roasted in the open field. It is used as a stuffing for vegetables and meats and mixed into salads. Freekeh is sold in Middle Eastern specialty shops, but you can use couscous, which also fluffs up well when cooked, as a suitable replacement.

INGREDIENTS

- 11 oz. (300 g) freekeh
- 1⅓ lb. (600 g) thin green asparagus
- 1 cup (30 g) finely chopped parsley
- 4 tbsp. extra virgin olive oil
- 2 garlic cloves, minced
- Juice of 1 lemon
- ½ tsp. finely chopped fresh green chili, deseeded
- 1 pinch salt
- 1 pinch freshly ground black pepper

DIRECTIONS

Wash freekeh well in a colander under running water.

Put freekeh in a bowl, cover with water and let soak for an hour, then drain.

Remove the woody, lower part of the asparagus spears and cut them into 1½-in. (3-cm) long pieces.

Fill a large bowl with ice water.

Bring water plus 1 tbsp. of salt to a boil in a large saucepan.

Blanch asparagus in the boiling water for 3 minutes.

Using a slotted spoon, transfer asparagus to the ice water to keep them green.

Add freekeh to the still-boiling water and cook for 5 minutes, until al dente.

Remove the freekeh, place it in a colander over a bowl, and drain well.

Drain asparagus, and squeeze gently to remove cooking water.

Mix freekeh and asparagus in a serving bowl, add the rest of the ingredients, toss, and serve.

LABANEH

Labaneh (pronounced "Lab-NEH") is a soft, tangy cheese made by straining yogurt. One of the most popular cheeses in the Middle East, it is combined with herbs (usually za'atar) for use as a dip, mixed into salads, and used in baking. Although often mistaken for Greek yogurt, labaneh can be strained further, so that it keeps its shape on the table, and rolled into balls, like mozzarella.

INGREDIENTS

1 qt. (1 l) full-fat Greek yogurt,
    preferably sheep's milk
1 tbsp. coarse salt
Extra virgin olive oil, to store

DIRECTIONS

Line a large bowl with a folded piece of cheesecloth or soft cotton fabric.
Combine yogurt and salt and pour into the lined bowl.
Pull cheesecloth corners up and tie them with a string to create a small bag.
Suspend in the air, directly above the bowl for 24 hours, to allow yogurt to drain.
Once drained, the labaneh should be smooth and thick. Serve it as-is, or store to use later.
To store, roll the labaneh into walnut-sized balls (using latex gloves to prevent contamination). Store in a jar full of olive oil.

GOOD TO KNOW

Use a mesh sieve that is slightly larger than the bowl to suspend the cheesecloth-wrapped yogurt over the bowl. Liquid will drain through the sieve and land in the bottom of the bowl, keeping it from touching your yogurt bundle.

ARUGULA SALAD WITH TOMATOES, LABANEH, AND SUMAC

A modern-day version of the classic jarjeer (watercress) salad, a staple of Arabic cuisine, this salad combines the acidity of tomatoes, the smooth, earthy flavor of labaneh, the citrusy taste of sumac, a spice made from ground red berries, and the complex flavors of the classic za'atar spice mix (of which sumac is a key ingredient) into a colorful, nuanced dish.

INGREDIENTS

2 bunches of washed and
 dried arugula leaves
 (preferably a wide-leaf variety)
4 ripe tomatoes
15 cherry tomatoes
1 red onion
6 balls of labaneh (page 42)
3 to 4 tbsp. za'atar spice mix
 (page 290)

Dressing
1 tsp. sumac (page 297)
2 tbsp. freshly squeezed
 lemon juice
3 tbsp. extra virgin olive oil
1 pinch salt
1 pinch freshly ground
 black pepper

DIRECTIONS

Slice the arugula leaves very thinly into 3-cm-wide strips.
Thinly slice both kinds of tomatoes.
Cut the onion lengthwise and then cut each half into thin half-moon shapes.
Roll the labaneh balls in the za'atar mix in a small bowl.
Combine the arugula leaves, sliced tomatoes, and onion in a large bowl.
Mix the sumac, lemon juice, olive oil, salt, and pepper in a small bowl.
Keep salad, labaneh balls, and dressing in separate bowls until just before serving.
When ready to eat, pour the dressing on the salad, toss gently, and top with labaneh balls.

WARM SPINACH SALAD WITH YOGURT DRESSING

In Galilee, it is customary to prepare warm and cold salads from wild winter greens like chicory, mallow, and spinach. This salad livens up what can be a common and even dull cooked green with the heat of green chili, the acidity of lemon, and the fresh zap of green onions. Yogurt binds it all together, making for a silky smooth and entirely satisfying side dish.

INGREDIENTS

Dressing
10 oz. (300 g) thick yogurt
2 garlic cloves, minced
2 tbsp. finely chopped
   mint leaves
3 tbsp. finely chopped green
   onions (white and green parts)
3 tbsp. extra virgin olive oil
2 tbsp. freshly squeezed
   lemon juice
1 pinch salt
1 pinch freshly ground
   black pepper

2 tbsp. unsalted butter
2 tbsp. extra virgin olive oil
2 garlic cloves, minced
½ tsp. finely chopped fresh
   green chili, deseeded
½ lb. (500 g) fresh spinach
   leaves, thoroughly washed
   and dried

DIRECTIONS

Place all the dressing ingredients in a bowl and mix well.
Cover the bowl and keep refrigerated.
Heat a saucepan over medium heat. Add butter and olive oil. Once the butter has melted, add garlic and chili and sauté for a few seconds, until garlic is golden. Be careful, as garlic can go from golden to burnt in a matter of seconds.
Add spinach leaves and sauté for 2 to 3 minutes, until the leaves soften slightly but are still firm.
Place the spinach and dressing in a serving bowl, mix gently, and serve.

BAKED EGGS

In Israel you will often find eggs baked into the fragrant tomato-and-pepper dish known as shakshuka. This recipe is even simpler, pairing vibrant fresh eggs baked in olive oil with the tanginess and deep red color of ground sumac. The dish was once baked in pottery, which spreads the heat evenly, but it can be made in a regular frying pan too.

INGREDIENTS

8 tbsp. extra virgin olive oil
4 eggs
2 tsp. sumac (page 297)
Salt and pepper to taste

DIRECTIONS

Preheat oven to 390°F (200°C).
Add 2 tbsp. of olive oil to each of 4 heat-resistant bowls.
Place bowls in the oven for 3 minutes to warm the oil.
Remove bowls and break an egg into each.
Sprinkle each bowl with ½ tsp. sumac and a little salt, then return to the oven for 4 minutes.
Using oven mitts, remove bowls from oven and serve each on a small plate to protect your tabletop from the heat.

LEVEL: ADVANCED

MAKES 6

MANAKEESH— FLATBREAD WITH TOPPINGS

Traditionally, this olive-oil-rich dough was rolled out and pressed with the fingertips, giving the dish its name (mankusha means "carving out" in Arabic). These tiny impressions ensured the toppings adhered to the dough. The flatbreads were then baked on the tava, a concave metal griddle placed over an open fire. The toppings were traditionally leftovers from poor households: sweet pepper spread, a za'atar/oregano mix, and onion fried with sumac.

INGREDIENTS

Dough
1 cup (500 g) white flour
1 tsp. fresh yeast
1⅓ cups (350 ml) water
2 tbsp. extra virgin olive oil
1 tbsp. sugar
1 tsp. salt

Sweet pepper spread
4 sweet red peppers
1 pinch salt
1 pinch freshly ground
    black pepper
1 tsp. olive oil for baking

Onion and sumac mix
3 tbsp. olive oil
3 onions, thinly sliced
1 tbsp. sumac
1 pinch salt
1 pinch freshly ground
    black pepper

Fresh oregano mix
1 cup (30 g) finely chopped
    fresh oregano leaves
2 garlic cloves, minced
½ tsp. lemon zest
3 tbsp. olive oil
1 pinch salt
1 pinch freshly ground
    black pepper

DIRECTIONS

Dough
Combine all dough ingredients in a standing mixer and knead with the dough hook for 3 minutes at low speed. Increase to medium speed and knead for another 5 minutes, until the dough is smooth and uniform. If you do not have a stand mixer with a dough hook, knead by hand for 8 minutes, until the dough becomes smooth and homogenous.
Place the dough in a lightly oiled bowl and cover with a clean dishtowel. Let rest at room temperature for two hours, or until dough doubles in size. About an hour before the dough is ready for baking, place a baking stone at the bottom of the oven and preheat to 480°F (250°C).
Once dough has risen, place on a floured work surface, divide into 6 equal portions, and roll each portion into a ball. Cover the balls with a clean dishtowel to prevent them from drying out.

Sweet pepper spread
Preheat oven to 430°F (220°C).
Place peppers on a roasting tray and roast them until the skins are charred. Using kitchen tongs, transfer to a large bowl, cover the bowl with plastic wrap, and allow to cool.
Peel the peppers, remove the seeds, and chop peppers finely.
Warm a non-stick saucepan (without oil) and add peppers. Season with salt and black pepper and cook over low heat, stirring constantly, until the mix becomes a red puree. Be careful not to singe the puree.

Onion and sumac mix
Warm olive oil in a large frying pan over high heat. Fry sliced onions until golden-brown. Add sumac and seasoning, stir well, and put in small bowl.

Fresh oregano mix
Mix all the ingredients together until well-blended.

Baking the manakeesh
After two hours of proofing, the dough should have doubled in size.
Flatten the 6 dough balls into 6 in. (15 cm) discs with your hands.
Spread the selected topping on each disc. Add a teaspoon of olive oil on top of each disc with the sweet pepper spread.
Using a lightly floured baker's peel, slide discs directly onto the baking stone and bake for 12 minutes.

GOOD TO KNOW

If you do not have a baking stone and a baker's peel, preheat the baking tray in the oven to create a hot surface and assemble your manakeesh on a sheet of baking paper to transfer it easily to the tray.

LAHM BI AJIN

Like the manakeesh flatbreads, this "Middle Eastern pizza" can be adjusted according to taste and seasonality. Beloved as an appetizer, a street snack, or as part of a large table of small dishes known as mezze, it is very common in Greater Syria and Southeastern Turkey, where it is called lahmacun. This popular regional version is topped with minced lamb and hot peppers.

INGREDIENTS

One quantity of manakeesh dough (page 50)

Filling
2 tbsp. extra virgin olive oil
2 small leeks, finely chopped
1 medium onion, finely chopped
2 garlic cloves
½ tsp. finely chopped
   fresh green chili, deseeded
½ tsp. finely chopped
   fresh red chili, deseeded
1 lb. (500 g) minced lamb
1 pinch salt
1 pinch freshly ground
   black pepper

DIRECTIONS

Make one quantity of manakeesh dough (page 50).
About an hour before the dough is ready for baking, place a baking stone in the bottom of the oven and preheat it to 480°F (250°C).
After the dough rises, scatter flour on your work surface, divide the dough into two equal portions, and roll each into a ball. Cover balls with a clean dishtowel to prevent from drying out.
Heat oil in a large frying pan and fry leeks, onion, garlic, and chilis until lightly golden.
Add the minced lamb and seasoning, and sauté just until the meat changes color. Transfer to a large bowl and allow to cool.
Roll out each ball of dough into a thin oval disc. Place each one on a lightly floured baker's peel and cover with topping mixture. Slide discs directly onto the baking stone and bake for 12 minutes.

GOOD TO KNOW

If you do not have a baking stone and a baker's peel, preheat the baking tray in the oven to create a hot surface, and assemble your lahm bi ajin on a sheet of baking paper to transfer easily to the tray.

ZA'ATAR PASTRY

The name za'atar refers to a wild herb (the leaves of the hyssop plant) as well as the spice mix made by combining its dried leaves with toasted sesame, sumac, and salt. Fresh and dried za'atar is a major symbol of the local cuisine with an unforgettable flavor. It is used in seasoning salads, cheeses, and baked goods like this pastry.

INGREDIENTS

Pastry
3½ cups (450 g) white flour
1⅓ cups (350 ml) cold water
½ tsp. dry yeast
1 tbsp. sugar
1 tbsp. olive oil
1 tsp. salt

Filling
1 cup (30 g) fresh za'atar
    (hyssop) or oregano leaves
2 tbsp. olive oil

DIRECTIONS

Combine the flour, water, yeast, and sugar in the bowl of a stand mixer and mix with the dough hook at slow speed for 3 minutes.
Add olive oil and salt, then mix at medium speed for another 5 minutes.
If you do not have a stand mixer with a dough hook, knead by hand for 8 minutes, until the dough becomes smooth and homogenous.
Place dough in a lightly oiled bowl and cover the bowl with a kitchen towel.
Let the dough rise at room temperature until it has doubled in size.
Once risen, divide the dough on a floured surface into 4 equal pieces.
Roll each into a ball and set them aside to rest for 15 minutes.
With a rolling pin, roll out each dough ball on a floured surface as thinly as possible.
Generously scatter fresh herbs onto each pastry sheet, drizzle a little olive oil on top, and fold into thirds.
You should end up with several layers of pastry with plenty of fresh leaves in the folds.
Let dough rest for another 15 minutes, then use a rolling pin to roll it out as thinly as possible again.
Heat a non-stick pan over high heat until hot and place the rolled-out pastry on it.
Dry-roast it for 3 minutes on each side, until golden brown.
Remove and serve while hot.

SOURDOUGH BREAD

Though intimidating to many, sourdough bread is actually rather easy and incredibly satisfying to bake at home. Once your starter is up and running and you have figured out your baking routine, it can become a wonderful ritual that fills the kitchen with a pleasing aroma and turns any house into a true home. The starter can be used indefinitely, as long as you keep feeding it every day or store it in the fridge for up to five days.

INGREDIENTS

3½ oz. (100 g) sourdough
    starter (page 294)
4 cups (500 g) bread flour
    (strong flour)
1⅓ cups (350 ml) water
1½ tsp. salt
1 tbsp. extra virgin olive oil

DIRECTIONS

Place all dough ingredients in the bowl of a standing mixer. Using the dough hook, knead for 3 minutes at low speed then at medium speed for another 5 minutes, until dough is smooth and uniform. If you do not have a stand mixer with a dough hook, knead by hand for 8 minutes, until the dough becomes smooth and homogenous.

Transfer dough to a lightly oiled bowl and cover the bowl with a clean dishtowel. Let the dough rest at room temperature for 2 hours, or until double in size.

On a floured work surface, roll the dough into a ball and then flatten slightly. Line a large bowl with a floured dish towel. Put the dough into the bowl and let rise for 4 to 5 hours, or until double in size.

About an hour before the dough is ready for baking, place a baking stone in the bottom of the oven and preheat the oven to 480°F (250°C) (see alternate methods below).

Invert the risen dough onto a floured baker's peel, use a sharp knife to score the dough (see below for scoring methods) and carefully slide the dough onto the baking stone. After 5 minutes, reduce the heat to 445°F (230°C) and bake for another 30 minutes.

Carefully take the loaf out of the oven and place it on a cooling rack. To make sure the bread is fully baked, turn the loaf over and tap it on the bottom. It should sound hollow, as if you were tapping on wood.

GOOD TO KNOW

If you do not have a baking stone and a baker's peel, preheat the baking tray in the oven to create a hot surface and use a sheet of baking paper to transfer the bread easily to the tray. Place a large baking dish full of water underneath the baking tray to create the requisite steam.

If you have a large, cast-iron pot, sometimes called a dutch oven, you can bake the sourdough bread using the California method: Simply place the covered, empty pot in the oven when you preheat. When the bread loaf is ready for baking, open the lid quickly, place the loaf inside, then cover again. After 30 minutes of baking, check the color of the bread. If not dark enough, continue to bake in 10-minute intervals with the pot's lid off, until a nice, dark brown crust is achieved.

Scoring (using a sharp knife or razor to make slits in the bread dough) is a crucial last step in the baking process and a way to control the shape of the final loaf. An unscored loaf will likely burst along its weakest point in the oven, and although still delicious, will not look very attractive. Every baker has a different method for scoring and a different preferred pattern. If you are a beginner, start with one line down the center of the loaf. A cross shape is also common, or you can experiment with a series of scores down the sides. In general, the more horizontal the scores, the further the bread crust will rise and separate, creating the attractive wings and grooves that are the mark of a professional loaf.

CALZONES WITH TZFATIT CHEESE

Every culture has its dumplings, and calzones are a popular dish in Sephardic communities around the world. The cheesy filling of these calzones comes from the kitchens of Safed and Tiberias, where women once made a pilgrimage to receive fertility blessings and returned with Tzfatit cheese, a hard, salty, aged sheep's milk cheese.

INGREDIENTS

Dough
4 cups (500 g) plain flour
8.5 fl. oz. (250 ml) cold water
1 tsp. fine salt
1 tsp. extra virgin olive oil

Filling
5 oz. (150 g) grated Tzfatit
    cheese, Pecorino Romano
    or any other hard sheep's
    milk cheese
4 oz. (100 g) ricotta
Freshly ground black pepper
    to taste

Serving
2 oz. (50 g) unsalted butter,
    at room temperature
1 tbsp. grated Tzfatit cheese,
    Pecorino Romano or any other
    hard sheep's milk cheese

DIRECTIONS

Using a food processer, pulse dough ingredients until they come together in a ball.
Remove the dough ball, cover with plastic wrap, and refrigerate for 30 minutes.
Place filling ingredients into a bowl and mix well.
On a floured work surface, roll refrigerated dough out to $\frac{1}{10}$ in. (3 mm) thick. Cut out small discs, about 4 in. (10 cm) in diameter. Place one teaspoon of filling at the center of each disc and fold it into a semicircle. Press the edges together and use the tongs of a fork to make small indentations on them.
In a large saucepan, add a pinch of salt to the water and bring to a boil. Add the calzones and cook for 6 minutes.
Using a slotted spoon or small sieve, remove calzones from the saucepan and place in a serving bowl. Add butter and wait until it melts to coat the calzones.
Sprinkle grated cheese on top and serve hot.

GOOD TO KNOW

If you do not have a round cookie-cutter, the round opening of an overturned cup or glass will work just as well for cutting out small discs.

NABLUS KUBBEH

Kubbeh, a stuffed dumpling made of bulgur or semolina, is a common dish in the Middle East, with dozens of versions. The Nablus kubbeh, named after the city of Nablus, is a type of fried kubbeh (as opposed to raw, steamed or broth-cooked kubbeh). On the coast, it is stuffed with fish or seafood instead of meat or vegetarian fillings.

INGREDIENTS

Dough
14 oz. (400 g) thin bulgur wheat
½ cup (85 g) semolina flour
1 tbsp. sweet paprika
1 egg, beaten
1 tsp. salt
½ tsp. freshly ground
   black pepper

Stuffing
11 oz. (300 g) white fish fillet,
   finely chopped or ground
   using a food processor
4 tbsp. finely chopped
   fresh parsley
1 tbsp. finely chopped
   fresh basil
½ tsp. lemon zest
½ tsp. salt
½ tsp. freshly ground
   black pepper

1 qt. (1 l) canola oil, for frying

DIRECTIONS

Place bulgur in a large bowl. Cover with 1 qt. (1l) of water and soak for 1 hour.
Strain bulgur and let dry in a strainer over a bowl for 1 hour.
Meanwhile, mix all stuffing ingredients except the oil in a large bowl until mixture is homogeneous and sticky. Refrigerate for 30 minutes.
In another bowl, mix bulgur and the rest of the dough ingredients. Using your hands, knead well until a homogeneous mixture solid enough to roll into balls forms.
Using slightly oiled hands, roll large balls out of the bulgur mixture, each roughly half the size of a tennis ball.
Place each ball in the center of your palm and use the thumb of your other hand to create a small dent in its center. Use your fingers to widen the dent until a small bowl forms.
Fill dough bowl with stuffing and push stuffing deep inside. Pull dough edges upwards and towards the center, gathering with your fingers until stuffing is completely surrounded. Roll back into a ball, making sure there are no cracks.
Roll each ball lengthwise until oval-shaped with pointed edges.
Line a plate with paper towels.
Heat canola oil in a pot over medium flame. Place kubbeh balls in the oil and fry until brown on all sides. Drain kubbeh on the plate. Serve warm.

FISH SENIYEH WITH TAHINI

This dish combines the typical ingredients of Greater Syrian cuisine—lemon, olive oil, herbs—and replaces hearty meats like lamb with the bounty of coastal communities. Here tahini, the sesame paste often mixed into hummus, is used as a hearty, earthy coating for the fish that thickens and browns up beautifully in the oven.

INGREDIENTS

2 onions, unpeeled
8 ripe tomatoes
2¼ lb. (1 kg) boneless, unskinned fillets of sea bass, black cod, grouper, or red snapper
½ cup (120 ml) extra virgin olive oil
1 hot red chili, finely chopped
1 tsp. grated lemon zest
½ tsp. ground fennel seed
1 pinch of ground cumin
¼ tsp. salt

Tahini
¾ cup (180 ml) raw tahini
1 cup (240 ml) cold water
Juice of ½ lemon
½ tsp. of fine salt

DIRECTIONS

Preheat oven to 480°F (250°C).
Arrange onions and tomatoes in baking dish and roast in the oven for 30 minutes until skins are charred, then remove to cool.
Once cool, chop coarsely and set aside.
Brush fish fillets with some olive oil and scatter chili, lemon zest, fennel seeds, cumin, and salt on top.
Heat olive oil in a frying pan. Add the fillets, skin side down, and fry for 6 minutes until skin becomes crisp and fillets no longer stick to the pan.
Carefully transfer fish to a roasting tray, skin side up, and arrange chopped vegetables on top.
Mix the tahini ingredients well until uniform and smooth, then pour tahini over the fish.
Roast in the oven for 10 to 12 minutes, until the tahini topping turns brown. Be careful not to over-roast, as the fish will dry out and the tahini will crack.

GOOD TO KNOW

A seniyeh is a low, round dish used for cooking, baking, and serving.
In the port towns of Acre and Jaffa it is often used for fish dishes, as well as for meat and vegetable dishes. If you do not have one, an earthenware casserole dish, a heavy pie dish, or an ovenproof pan will work just as well.

TIBERIAS-STYLE FRIED GEFILTE FISH PATTIES

A rich and fascinating cuisine evolved in Tiberias, a city where Jews, Muslims, and Christians lived side by side for thousands of years. These gefilte fish patties came from Jews emigrating from Poland in the eighteenth century, but it was their Sephardic neighbors who added local seasoning and decided to fry them, creating a unique twist on a dish served at Passover all over the world.

INGREDIENTS

1 lb. (500 g) freshwater fish (carp, pike, or whitefish), skinned and deboned
1 onion, finely chopped
9 oz. (250 g) pumpkin, peeled and finely grated
2 tbsp. extra virgin olive oil
1 tsp. fine sea salt
1 tsp. freshly ground pepper
½ cup (120 ml) mild olive oil, for frying
1 carrot, peeled and thinly sliced, for garnishing
1 lemon, halved, for garnishing

DIRECTIONS

Chop fish finely, by hand or with a meat grinder (using the coarse plate). Place fish in a bowl and add the onion, pumpkin, olive oil, salt, and pepper. Mix well until uniform. Knead the mixture like dough for 5 minutes, until it becomes sticky.
Refrigerate for at least an hour until slightly firm.
Heat olive oil in a large frying pan. Oil your hands slightly and roll egg-sized patties from the fish mix. Flatten slightly, then slide carefully into the pan.
Fry the patties on both sides until golden, then remove and drain on a plate covered with a dish towel.
Gently sauté the carrot slices until soft.
Arrange the patties on a serving dish, place a slice of fried carrot on each one, and serve accompanied with half a lemon.

GRILLED GROUPER WITH WHITE WINE, BUTTERNUT SQUASH, AND OLIVE OIL

On the eastern shores of the Mediterranean Sea, grouper is considered the king of fish. Its meaty, juicy flesh can take on a lot of flavor without losing its own distinct personality. In this dish, it fits just right with the sweetness of butternut squash, a modern addition to the area's traditional vegetables. Served in a roasting tray straight from the oven, it makes a dramatic impression.

INGREDIENTS

1 butternut squash, unpeeled
4 tbsp. extra virgin olive oil
1 tsp. coarse sea salt
Freshly ground black pepper
    to taste
1 red onion, sliced into thin rings
1 whole grouper or sea bass,
    weighing around 2 lb. (1 kg)
1 tsp. finely chopped
    oregano leaves, plus 4 sprigs
½ tsp. grated lemon zest
2 cloves of garlic, minced

DIRECTIONS

Preheat oven to 480°F (250°C).
Cut the butternut squash in half lengthwise and remove the seeds with a tablespoon.
Cut the halves into slices ¾ in. (2 cm) thick.
Place slices on a baking tray, drizzle with 2 tbsp. of olive oil and season with salt and black pepper. Roast for 20 minutes, or until butternut squash is soft and slightly brown.
Meanwhile, place onion rings in a roasting tray and drizzle with 2 tbsp. of olive oil. When the butternut squash is soft, remove from the oven (leaving oven on) and add the slices to the roasting tray on top of the onion rings.
Place the fish on a chopping board. Using a sharp knife, make a cut along one side from head to tail.
Combine chopped oregano leaves, lemon zest, and garlic in a small bowl. Using your fingers, stuff the mix into the opened side of the fish.
Place fish on top of the onions and roasted butternut squash, with the cut facing up if possible. Arrange the oregano sprigs in the tray, season with salt and pepper, and cover with aluminum foil.
Roast for 15 minutes, then remove aluminum foil and roast uncovered for an additional 7 to 8 minutes.

SAYADIEH— FISH WITH RICE

Originally made from cheap cuts and scraps that would not otherwise be sold to traders, sayadieh is a classic fishermen's dish of fish, seafood, and rice. Presented at the table on a large metal platter, it is ladled onto each diner's plate, covered with tahini, and accompanied by a finely chopped vegetable salad, like the Acre-Style Vegetable Salad (page 38).

INGREDIENTS

2 cups (400 g) basmati or other good quality long-grain rice

3 tbsp. extra virgin olive oil

1 onion, finely chopped

3 cloves of garlic, minced

14 oz. (400 g) calamari, cut into ⅓ in. (1 cm) rings

½ tsp. ground turmeric

1 tsp. coarse sea salt

1 qt. (1 l) fish stock (page 286)

1⅓ lb. (600 g) boneless fillets of firm white-fleshed fish (such as sea bass, black cod, grouper, red snapper)

1 tsp. chopped pistachio nuts, for garnishing

DIRECTIONS

Rinse the rice in a colander under running water. Then place colander over a bowl to drain.

Heat olive oil in a wide saucepan. Add onion and garlic and fry until the onion turns brown. Add the calamari and mix well.

Add the rice and sauté it, stirring constantly for 2 minutes, until rice grains are coated with oil and the edges are slightly transparent. Add turmeric, salt, and fish stock and mix well.

Place the fillets in the saucepan, mix gently, and cover. Reduce the heat to the lowest possible setting and simmer for 25 minutes.

Remove the saucepan from the heat and let stand, still covered, for 15 minutes.

Divide into individual serving bowls or transfer to one large serving bowl. Garnish with chopped pistachio nuts and serve.

ROASTED LAMB CHOPS

Lamb is one of Israel's most popular meats, especially delectable when sourced from locally reared animals (rich in fat with a strong, dominant flavor). Lamb chops are usually roasted on a charcoal grill or in the oven. Their flavor is so distinctive it does not need much enhancement aside from a simple mixture of fresh herbs.

INGREDIENTS

12 thick lamb chops, bone exposed and fat removed

Herb rub
½ cup (15 g) chopped fresh parsley
2 tbsp. thyme
1 tsp. chopped fresh oregano
1 tsp. lemon zest
3 garlic cloves, finely chopped
3 tbsp. olive oil
½ tsp. coarse salt
1 tsp. freshly ground black pepper

DIRECTIONS

Preheat oven to 430°F (220°C).
Heat a roasting pan over high heat, until it is blazing.
Sear lamb chops for 2 minutes on each side and set aside.
Combine herb rub ingredients in a bowl and mix well until the mixture has the texture of wet sand.
Arrange lamb chops on a flat roasting tray. Sprinkle one heaping tablespoon of the herb rub on one side of each chop and press into the meat.
Roast in the oven for 6 to 8 minutes, until medium rare.
Let the lamb chops cool for 5 minutes before serving.

MASAKHAN— ROASTED CHICKEN WITH ONION

Masakhan is a definitive Arab dish served during the olive harvest, featuring roast chicken with onion rings on an olive-oil drenched pita or manakeesh (page 50). Its name derives from the word sakhneh (Arabic for "hot") in Ramallah. In Galilee, it is called muhmar from the word akhmar (Arabic for "red"), which refers to the reddish tone of the sumac.

INGREDIENTS

2 small whole chickens,
    2–3⅓ lb. (1–1½ kg) each
¾ cup (180 ml) olive oil
5 onions, sliced into thin strips
Salt and pepper to taste
1 pita or manakeesh (page 50)

DIRECTIONS

Dry-roast the chickens in a heavy, ovenproof casserole dish or cast-iron pot until lightly browned.
Remove chickens and set aside.
Add olive oil and onions to the casserole dish and sauté over low heat until onions are golden brown.
Add chicken, season with salt and pepper, cover, and roast for one hour at 375°F (190°C).
Remove lid and continue baking uncovered for another 20 minutes.
Take casserole out of the oven and let stand for 10 minutes.
Serve on a slice of pita or manakeesh (page 50) doused with olive oil, allowing the juices to run into the bread and the flavors to set.

LUBIYA (BLACK-EYED PEAS) WITH LAMB

A recipe inspired by festive Sephardic meals served for the New Year, lubiya is eaten all over the Middle East and particularly beloved in Egypt. Black-eyed peas and lamb play a major role in this dish, but the fresh herbs give it a special flair. They are particularly evocative of the landscape of this fertile region bursting with green.

INGREDIENTS

3 tbsp. extra virgin olive oil

3 garlic cloves, minced

1 red chili, roughly chopped

½ lb. (250 g) plum tomatoes, halved

½ lb. (250 g) ripe red vine tomatoes, quartered

Fresh basil leaves, from 2 sprigs

Salt and pepper to taste

1 lb. (450 g) fresh black-eyed peas

4 tbsp. finely chopped fresh parsley

4 tbsp. finely chopped fresh coriander

1 lb. (450 g) lamb meat, thinly sliced

2 tbsp. spring onions, chopped, for garnishing

DIRECTIONS

Place the olive oil, garlic, and chili in a heavy-based saucepan over high heat and sauté lightly.

Add both kinds of tomatoes, basil, salt, and pepper, and cook over medium-high heat, stirring occasionally.

Once the mixture comes to a boil, reduce heat and simmer for ten minutes until tomatoes soften and release their juices.

Remove saucepan from heat and pass contents through a coarse sieve placed over a bowl. Use a wooden spoon to press the tomatoes through, extracting all their juices.

Transfer sauce to a clean saucepan and continue to simmer over low heat.

In another large saucepan, bring 1½ qt. (1½ l) of water with 3 tbsp. salt to a boil. (Do not skimp on the salt—the water must be salty).

When the water comes to a boil, add black-eyed peas and cook for 5 to 6 minutes.

Remove black-eyed peas with a slotted spoon, add to the sauce, and then add parsley and coriander.

Mix well and let simmer for 15 to 20 minutes.

While sauce is simmering, season the lamb slices with salt and pepper, then sprinkle a little olive oil over them.

Heat a heavy frying pan and fry lamb slices for 2 minutes on each side.

Transfer lamb to a cutting board and cut into thin strips with a sharp knife.

Add thin strips to the saucepan with the black-eyed peas and stir well.

Garnish with chopped spring onions and serve.

DATE AND ALMOND MAAMOUL

A bit like a stuffed shortbread, maamoul are traditional filled cookies made with a crumbly, semolina-based dough, filled with any number of dried fruits and nuts, and even accented with orange blossom water. They are often made in Arab households to mark the end of Ramadan, but any celebratory occasion would be well served by their presence on the table.

INGREDIENTS

Dough
7 oz. (200 g) white flour
3½ oz. (100 g) semolina
7 oz. (200 g) unsalted butter, in ¾ in. (2 cm) cubes
1 egg
2 tbsp. powdered sugar
1 pinch of fine salt
½ tsp. baking powder

Filling
11 oz. (300 g) Medjool dates, pitted and finely chopped
7 oz. (200 g) almonds, unblanched and coarsely ground
2 to 3 drops orange-blossom extract

Powdered sugar for dusting

DIRECTIONS

Using a food processer, pulse dough ingredients until they come together in a ball.
Remove the dough ball, cover in plastic wrap, and refrigerate for an hour.
Meanwhile, combine all filling ingredients in a bowl and mix well.
Preheat oven to 350°F (180°C).
Divide dough into 20 equal portions. With lightly oiled hands, form each portion into a ball and then flatten the balls into discs 1½ in. (4 cm) in diameter. Place ½ tsp. of filling in each.
Fold discs around the filling, then roll them back into balls, taking care not to let the filling get squeezed out.
Line a baking tray with baking paper. Place the balls on the tray. Gently press them to create a slightly flattened circle.
Using tweezers, carefully make small pinches on one flat surface, creating any pattern you wish. Take care not to expose the filling.
Bake for 25 minutes, until cookies are baked but not browned.
Remove and let cool.
Dust cookies with powdered sugar and store in an airtight container.

GOOD TO KNOW

Traditionally, maamoul are made with a wooden mold, giving them their patterned ridges and spikes. Here we have offered a by-hand approximation of this process, for those who may not have such a mold.

DATE AND ALMOND BAKLAVA

The classic flaky pastry known as baklava is a dessert that seems to transcend all boundaries of race, religion, and nationality. This version has almonds, dates, and the distinctive fragrance of orange blossom water, but others include pistachio and honey. Whatever you do not eat can be stored in an airtight container for days or frozen for months, but it is best when fresh.

INGREDIENTS

2 lb. (1 kg) readymade
   puff pastry
14 oz. (400 g) pitted Medjool
   dates, finely chopped
10 oz. (300 g) almonds,
   unblanched and coarsely
   ground
2–3 drops orange blossom
   extract
1 egg, beaten, for brushing
3 tbsp. muscovado sugar

Syrup
⅓ cup (75 g) white sugar
⅓ cup (80 ml) water

DIRECTIONS

Preheat oven to 430°F (220°C).
Line a rectangular baking tray, 9 × 13 in. (23 × 33 cm), with baking paper.
On a floured work surface, roll the pastry until it is ¹⁄₁₀ in. (3 mm) thick.
Divide it into two halves and use one half to line the tray.
Combine the dates, almonds, and orange blossom extract in a bowl.
Spread the mixture evenly over the pastry in the baking tray. Place the second half of the pastry on top and lightly press it onto the filling.
Brush the beaten egg over the pastry. With a sharp knife, make diamond-shaped scores on its surface.
Scatter muscovado sugar on top of the baklava and bake for 22 minutes.
Meanwhile, combine syrup ingredients in a small saucepan and bring to a boil over medium heat.
Once the baklava is browned, take it out of the oven. Pour syrup evenly over the baklava and let it cool to room temperature. Using a sharp knife, cut baklava into pieces, using the diamond scores as your guide.
Best eaten at room temperature.

POACHED PEARS IN WHITE WINE

A very elegant, "grown up" dessert, poached pears are a deceptively simple dish—their relatively short ingredient list and straightforward presentation belie the complex flavors within. Fairly light as far as sweet dishes go, they are also the perfect end to a languid, multi-course meal, when your guests are too full for a baked dessert but a simple piece of fruit just won't do.

INGREDIENTS

6 firm but ripe Bosc or
   Anjou pears
1 bottle of dry white wine
2 tbsp. brown sugar
Zest of half a lemon
4 whole cloves
1 sprig of lemon verbena
4 tbsp. crème fraîche, for serving

DIRECTIONS

Peel the pears, cut in half lengthwise, and core using a Parisian spoon, grapefruit spoon, or melon baller.
Combine all the ingredients except the crème fraîche in a large saucepan.
Cover the pan and bring the mixture to a boil over high heat.
Once the mixture begins to boil, remove the lid and continue cooking until the wine has almost entirely evaporated and there is a pale caramel syrup at the bottom of the saucepan.
Remove saucepan from the heat and allow to cool for 20 minutes.
Serve with a tablespoon of crème fraîche on each dish.

GOOD TO KNOW

Fresh lemon verbena is hard to find, but a revelation. Dried can be an adequate substitute, but do not expect the same knockout punch of flavor.

QUINCE TARTE TATIN

With its unusual appearance—gnarled, fuzzy, and overgrown—and surprising aroma, the quince is one of the world's strangest yet most satisfying fruits. Baked quince is a beloved traditional dessert in Jewish-Sephardic and Jewish-Balkan cuisines, and is even paired with savory flavors in Middle Eastern dishes. Here, quince replaces apple in a classic tarte tatin.

INGREDIENTS

7 oz. (200 g) unsalted butter
6 oz. (170 g) white sugar
6 quinces, peeled, cored,
   and quartered
¼ cup (60 ml) water
2 cinnamon sticks
2 lb. (1 kg) readymade,
   all-butter puff pastry

DIRECTIONS

Preheat oven to 375°F (190°C).
Place a 10 in. (26 cm) ovenproof frying pan on the stove over medium heat. Add butter and sugar and cook, stirring constantly, until sugar dissolves and caramel turns a dark amber color.
Remove the pan from the heat and let cool slightly.
Arrange the quartered quinces on the frying pan, cut-side down. Pour ¼ cup (60 ml) of water over them and place cinnamon sticks between them. Cover the pan with two layers of aluminum foil, place in the oven, and bake for 40 minutes. Check quinces' tenderness. If quinces are still firm, bake for another 10 minutes.
Remove pan from the oven and reduce the temperature to 350°F (180°C). Remove aluminum foil and let pan cool for 10 minutes.
On a floured work surface, roll out the puff pastry until ⅕ in. (5 mm) thick. Cover the pan with the pastry, cutting off any excess. Place in the oven and bake for 20 minutes or until pastry is browned.
Remove from oven. Place large serving dish over pan and carefully invert. Allow it to cool for 10 minutes and serve warm.

GOOD TO KNOW

Like apples and pears, quinces tend to oxidize quickly once peeled. To avoid browned and generally unattractive quince quarters, set aside a bowl of water with a squeeze of half a lemon while prepping and place each quince quarter in the water until ready to use.

FIG AND MASCARPONE TART

One of the Biblical Seven Species (page 296), figs have been one of Israel's most important fruits for millennia. Their growth and export powered the region's economy, and their sweet, earthy taste makes them a beloved feature of many Middle Eastern desserts. You can bake this delicious tart either in a 9½-in. (24-cm) baking tin or as individual desserts in four 4¾-in. (12-cm) tins.

INGREDIENTS

Pastry
10½ oz. (300 g) plain flour
7 oz. (200 g) unsalted butter
1 egg
2 tbsp. powdered sugar
1 pinch of fine salt

Filling
11 oz. (300 g) mascarpone cheese
½ tsp. lemon zest
A few drops of vanilla extract
1 tbsp. powdered sugar,
plus more for dusting
1 lb. (500 g) fresh figs

DIRECTIONS

Using a food processer, pulse pastry ingredients until they come together in a ball.

Remove the dough ball, cover in plastic wrap, and refrigerate for an hour.

Meanwhile, mix all filling ingredients, except for the figs, in a bowl.

Preheat oven to 350°F (180°C).

On a floured work surface, roll out the pastry into a disc approx. 1/10 in. (3 mm) thick and 6½ in. (16 cm) in diameter.

Drape pastry over the tart tin. Every baker has a favored method for getting the rolled pastry from the work surface into the tart tin in one piece.

You can drape it over the rolling pin and then lift it up, or fold it gently into fourths, transfer it, and then unfold again when it is securely in the tin.

Press down with your fingertips so the pastry adheres to the tin.

Use a sharp knife to remove any excess pastry.

Place a sheet of baking paper on top of the pastry and fill it with ceramic pie weights. If you do not have ceramic pie weights, any kind of dry legume will work. Beans with heft and a waxy surface, like butter beans or lima beans, are ideal.

Bake for 16 minutes, or until the edges of the tart turn golden.

Remove tart from the oven and let it cool completely.

Remove pie weights (which can be reused) and baking paper.

Pour the mascarpone filling onto the pastry and smooth it using a knife, spatula, or cake icer.

Slice figs and arrange on top, either at random or in a pattern of your choosing.

Dust with powdered sugar and serve.

TEL AVIV

**TEL AVIV—
COOKING IN THE
MELTING POT**

Tel Aviv's strategic location—right on the Mediterranean coast and in the center of the country—makes it an obvious culinary destination. With access to the best produce from the four corners of the country, plus whatever the sea yields, it was always primed to be both a cultural and culinary melting pot. Today it is also Israel's center of culinary innovation, where chefs go to find inspiration, build their careers, and really wow their hungry guests.

Israel's gleaming, modern metropolis has always enjoyed an exciting reputation. But while young and trend-conscious visitors used to flock to its beaches and clubs, now they're drawn by ambitious, innovative chefs looking to make their mark. Always forward-thinking, ever artistic, Tel Aviv's cuisine spans centuries and continents, and now it's making an international splash.

Tastes have shifted with the decades and younger generations are more interested in what is new, different, and global.

Above: **Boaz Peled, chef and restaurant owner, often serves arak, the local anise-based drink, with his fish dishes.** Below: **Turkish burek, a popular pastry in Tel Aviv, sliced up into bite-sized pieces at the Levinsky Market.**

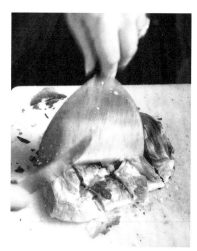

With its gleaming towers, glamorous beaches, and thousands of Bauhaus gems, Tel Aviv is a decidedly modern city. It did not always look that way, though. In fact, a little over 100 years ago, it was not much more than a sand dune next to an ancient Arab center of trade—the port of Jaffa. Then, with a vision of an all-Jewish city, David Ben-Gurion and his followers christened this place "Tel Aviv," which literally means "Hill of Spring." The name also pays clever homage to Theodor Herzl's utopian novel Altneuland (meaning "old new land" in German)—the "tel" in Tel Aviv references layered hills of artifacts, while "aviv" can also mean "growth" or "revival."

The city was established in 1909 by Jewish immigrants hoping to start a new life. In fledgling Tel Aviv, the languages heard on the street were mostly Polish,

When red mullet is this fresh, it only needs a slice of lemon on the side and a glass of arak. (See recipe on p. 132)

Sandwiches can be traditional or contemporary. This succulent example from Dallal restaurant in the fashionable Neve Tzedek district tops freshly cooked spinach with a poached egg and fish roe. Opposite page: Enjoying a quick bite of a classic dish: falafel in pita.

Cosmopolitan Tel Aviv has everything—
espresso bars, pizzerias, Chinese restaurants, and burger joints—but many diners
still enjoy its locally made hummus.

INTRODUCING…
THE TABUN OVEN

All over the world you can find
civilizations that have used wood,
coal, or clay to cook for generations. Some of them even bury
their food in the ground and let
the trapped heat do the work.
The tabun employs some of these
methods, featuring a clay oven
with a hole at the bottom for
stoking fires and a hole at the top
that can be covered with a lid.
It has been used for centuries by
Palestinians for breads, stews, and
all manner of meaty, savory dishes.

Yiddish, and German, and the cuisine reflected these countries as well. There
were many meat-and-potato-based dishes that look a lot like what can be
found in Eastern Europe today. Remnants of the old world still pop up in
contemporary Tel Aviv—little restaurants serving classic Ashkenazi dishes like
chicken soup, gefilte fish, and jellied calves' feet—but for the most part tastes
have shifted with the decades, and younger generations are more interested in
what is new, different, and global.

Those looking to understand the city's culinary evolution would do best to
look back th the 1940s, to a time when floods of Jews were arriving in Palestine
during and after the horrors of the Second World War. In the late 1940s, Jewish
immigrants from Yemen had also just arrived in the city. In neighborhoods like
Kerem Hateimanim (literally, "Yemenites' Vineyard") and Hatikva, eateries
abound that still serve soup cooked on kerosene stoves alongside dough and
bread specialties from Yemenite Jewish cuisine. Jews from the Balkans made
later additions to the melting pot. They arrived as the region opened up to the
world after the Cold War, then plunged into its own civil war in the 1990s.
The newcomers opened modest restaurants serving their own traditional dishes, further additions to the region's rich culinary fabric.

Restaurants run by Mizrahi (Jews of Eastern origin) offered menus featuring
their own set of traditional dishes, including skewers of grilled meat, hummus, and salads. But by the 1970s, Israelis were seeking inspiration far beyond
the Mediterranean. A multitude of new establishments opened in Tel Aviv, including espresso bars, pizzerias, Chinese restaurants, and burger joints, further
defining it as a global culinary capital on par with New York City—home to
another thriving Jewish population.

Israeli chefs may get their produce from the north and their fish from the Mediterranean, but they come to Tel Aviv to make a name for themselves.

A diner uses doughy
bread to soak up
shakshuka. Opposite
page, top. Cooks
at Ha'kosem dish up
the day's delicacies.
Opposite page, bottom:
The scene in front
of Da Da & Da, a tren-
dy new restaurant
on Rothschild Blvd.

By the 1970s, Israelis were seeking inspiration beyond the Mediterranean. Their explorations and innovations helped define Tel Aviv as a global culinary capital on a par with New York City.

INTRODUCING…
THE SESAME SEED

Middle Eastern cuisine simply would not be the same without this tiny, humble speck of a seed. In this chapter alone, you will find it sprinkled on focaccia (page 122) or made into halva for the chocolate and halva pastry (page 152). In its liquid form—tahini—it features prominently in many recipes, either as the foundation of a dish (hummus and tahini), or just as a drizzle to garnish the plate before serving. It may come as a shock, then, to find that sesame seeds are not grown in Israel, but rather imported in bulk from Africa and India. Once here, however, they are processed into the pastes and sauces beloved by Israelis, Palestinians, and, more recently, international diners.

Yomi Levi, third-generation Jewish-Turkish merchant, proudly shows off the wide spectrum of olive types and colors at his family's shop in the Levinsky Market.

Jaffa is an ancient fishing center, its picturesque old port home to fishing boats that provide much of the country's fresh catch.

The current food revolution started taking shape in the late 1980s. Young chefs, the grandchildren of immigrants, went abroad to study professionally, serving as apprentices in famous restaurants across Europe and the United States. Returning to Israel, they drew on ancestral cooking traditions and merged them with current trends and methods. Raw ingredients like olive oil, local fish, and an impressive array of fruits and vegetables were given particular emphasis. Jews looking to expand their food horizons and connect with their geographic neighbors found inspiration in Palestinian cuisine, which, of course, had been there all along. Contemporary Mediterranean cuisine in Israel, created mostly in Tel Aviv and the central region, is grounded in the use of fresh ingredients with minimal treatment and local techniques such as charcoal grilling or baking in a traditional tabun oven (more information on page 92).

This page: **Some fishing families go back generations, with fathers and sons working side by side.** Opposite page: **Fishermen and fish merchants strike a bargain at Dallal.**

Port cities, once economic and governmental centers and places where goods and knowledge were exchanged, have always been famed for their cuisine.

The evolution of Jaffa's cuisine, on the other hand, is much harder to trace, though the city has been part of recorded history for thousands of years. Port cities, once economic and governmental centers and places where goods and knowledge were exchanged, have always been famed for their cuisine. After the foundation of the state of Israel concluded a lengthy war in 1948, only a handful of families remained in Jaffa. Most became refugees, dispersed throughout the Middle East. Old houses, as well as newer, rapidly built housing projects, were taken over by families of Arab refugees fleeing other areas and by Jewish refugees arriving after 1948. Of course, everyone brought their own cuisine and eating habits, and eventually, restaurants came to celebrate different eras in the region's culinary evolution and varied gastronomic backgrounds—sometimes all on one plate.

Today, Jaffa and Tel Aviv share the same municipal authority, and Jaffa is still a busy fishing center, its picturesque old port still home to fishing boats providing much of the country's fresh catch. Its hummus joints are also famous throughout the country. More recently, local cooks have begun tracing the legacy of Jaffa's cuisine, reconstructing nearly forgotten recipes with the help of women from the oldest families in town. Numerous farmers' markets have sprung up in Tel Aviv and Jaffa, offering produce from all over Israel. Pilgrims and storytellers spoke of Jaffa as an important citrus-growing area for centuries. The small-town-turned-metropolis was indeed once surrounded by fields and citrus groves. In the mid-nineteenth century, for example, the farmers of Jaffa discovered the Shamouti orange, later known as the Jaffa orange, and Arab and Jewish growers began exporting it overseas. Although today many orange groves have been uprooted by rapid urbanization, the Sharon region north of Tel Aviv remains an important hub for growing and exporting citrus varieties, and the sweet and sour taste of citrus still dominates the region's cuisine.

CONTROVERSIAL SEAFOOD

Kosher law dictates that to be eaten, fish must have scales and fins. That would make all shellfish forbidden in the Jewish kitchen. Yet these days, there are plenty of crabs, lobsters, shrimp, and scallops on the menus. What happened? According to *Haaretz*, Israel's independent daily newspaper, the fad for decidedly non-kosher shellfish began in the 1980s and peaked in the mid-1990s, when shellfish imports were officially allowed into Israel and restaurants began to cater to a growing tourism industry.

Local cooks have begun tracing the legacy of Jaffa's cuisine, and numerous farmers' markets have sprung up all across Tel Aviv.

Nowadays, Tel Aviv is the most forward thinking, liberal, and contemporary of Israel's towns and cities, indisputably its cultural and culinary capital. Built up from the sand, a blank slate waiting to become its own Jewish utopia, Tel Aviv was primed for its current role: it is just so much easier to dare and innovate when tradition is lacking. While its buildings whisper of 100 years of modernist history, Tel Aviv is truly the flagship of Israel's new cuisine. The streets of this metropolis on the Mediterranean are home to some of the country's finest restaurants and a vibrant food scene, attracting gourmets from all over the world. Israeli chefs may get their produce from the north, their fish from the Mediterranean, but they come here to make a name for themselves, and to make the rest of the world sit up and take notice.

Carmel Market, the covered farmer's market at Tel Aviv port, sells just about everything a home cook or professional chef could want at its many family-owned stalls.

TASTE OF INNOV- ATION

Recipes from Tel Aviv include fresh salads and grains, modern takes on focaccia, and colorful celebrations of fresh produce that put vegetables front and center. There are some old Eastern European favorites as well as dishes that would be more at home in China or Japan. One thing is certain, the chefs in Tel Aviv are always innovating—and with a bit of inspiration, you can too.

Roasted artichokes, with tomato vinaigrette, Parmesan cream, Parmesan shavings, and chimichurry, served at the Dallal restaurant in Tel Aviv.

LEAF SALAD WITH ORANGES AND PARMESAN

A green salad with citrus fruit and cheese shavings makes a lovely appetizer or second course. Its colors brighten up the table and its flavors meld the sharpness of hard cheese with the tanginess of citrus layered with pleasingly aromatic herbs. Such salads are often a lot easier than they look, making them the perfect last-minute accompaniment to a feast.

INGREDIENTS

Juice of 1 orange
½ tsp. orange zest
2 tbsp. olive oil
1 tsp. fine salt
½ tsp. freshly ground
  black pepper
3 tbsp. fresh mint leaves
3 tbsp. fresh parsley leaves
1 handfull fresh arugula leaves
2 oranges, segmented,
  without membranes and seeds
¼ cup (25 g) grated Parmesan
  cheese

DIRECTIONS

Combine the orange juice, orange zest, oil, salt, and pepper in a small bowl and mix well.
Place half of the mint, parsley, and arugula leaves in a salad bowl.
Top the leaves with half of the orange segments.
Repeat the ast two steps.
Pour the dressing on top, sprinkle on the Parmesan cheese shavings, and serve.

FENNEL SALAD

Quick-pickled fennel is popular in many North African cuisines, where it is served as a refreshing addition to heavy and complex couscous dishes. Combined with other cold vegetable dishes (like Leaf Salad with Oranges and Parmesan), page 107, and Beetroot Carpaccio, page 110), this version can be part of a fantastic meze spread, each component a small celebration of the fruits of the land.

INGREDIENTS

4 medium fennel bulbs, trimmed
Juice of 3 lemons
1 tsp. finely chopped fresh
    red Anaheim chili peppers,
    deseeded
1 tsp. fine salt
2 tbsp. olive oil
2 thyme stalks, for garnishing

DIRECTIONS

Halve the fennel bulbs lengthwise.
Place the halves on a cutting board, cut side down, and slice lengthwise into ⅕-in.-thick (½-cm-thick) strips.
Combine fennel strips with lemon juice, chili, and salt in a bowl.
Mix well.
Refrigerate for 2 hours, then mix again and arrange on a serving dish.
Drizzle the olive oil over the fennel, garnish with thyme, and serve.

RAW BEETROOT CARPACCIO

Beef and tuna carpaccio have long been essential parts of Italian cuisine, but at some point, vegetarians took note. The method of slicing meat very thinly enhances its flavor and allows it to soak up sauces and dressings particularly well, so why not use it with vegetables? This beetroot carpaccio has a particularly silken texture, its earthy flavor accented with acidity and spice.

INGREDIENTS

2 raw beets, peeled
3 tbsp. pomegranate juice
1 tbsp. freshly squeezed
   lemon juice
2 tbsp. extra virgin olive oil
1 tsp. coarse salt
½ tsp. freshly ground
   black pepper
¼ cup (40 g) pomegranate
   seeds
1 tbsp. fresh oregano leaves
1 red Anaheim chili,
   deseeded and chopped

DIRECTIONS

Use a mandoline slicer to slice the beets into 1-mm-thin slices.
Combine the pomegranate juice, lemon juice, oil, salt, and pepper in a small bowl and mix well.
Arrange the beet slices on a serving dish so they are close together, but not overlapping.
Pour the dressing over the carpaccio and scatter the pomegranate seeds, oregano leaves, and chili over the dressing.
Let the carpaccio sit for 10 minutes so it absorbs the dressing, then serve.

ROASTED RED CABBAGE

Red cabbage has been a staple of Ashkenazi Jewish cuisine in western and northern Europe for generations. Here it is given the Mediterranean treatment, pairing its sharpness with olive oil, pomegranate juice, and walnuts, and drawing out its flavor by quickly roasting it in a pan. This is definitely not your grandmother's cabbage anymore.

INGREDIENTS

1 medium head of red cabbage
3 tbsp. olive oil
1 tsp. coarse salt
½ tsp. freshly ground
   black pepper

Dressing
3 tbsp. pomegranate juice
2 tbsp. olive oil
2 tbsp. chopped parsley
½ tsp. fine salt
2 tbsp. crushed walnuts,
   for garnishing

DIRECTIONS

Cut the cabbage in half, then cut each half into slices roughly ¾ in. (2 cm) thick.
Make sure to leave enough of the stem to hold the cabbage leaves together.
Heat a heavy skillet until smoking hot.
Brush cabbage slices with olive oil and season well with salt and pepper.
Roast one slice at a time in the skillet, 5–7 minutes on each side, until slightly charred.
Place cooked slices in a serving bowl.
Mix all dressing ingredients except the walnuts in a small bowl.
Pour the dressing over the cabbage, garnish with walnuts, and serve.

LEEK CONFIT

Though often banished to the bottom of a soup pot, or used along with garlic and onions simply to flavor a dish, leeks are remarkably delicious vegetables that make for a satisfying meal on their own. Slow roasting in the oven turns them brown and caramelized, until they are as succulent and appetizing as fall-off-the-bone meat roasts—and just as satisfying.

INGREDIENTS

6 baby leeks
2 tbsp. olive oil
½ tsp. fine salt
½ tsp. freshly ground
  black pepper
½ qt. (½ l) chicken (page 289)
  or vegetable stock (page 286)

DIRECTIONS

Preheat oven to 390°F (200°C).
Slice the leeks into 1–2-in.-long (3–5-cm-long) sections and arrange in a deep roasting tray.
Drizzle with olive oil and season with salt and pepper.
Roast for 20 minutes, until the leeks are lightly golden.
Add stock, reduce oven temperature to 320°F (160°C), and roast for about 40 minutes, until leeks are browned and tender and the stock has been absorbed. (If some liquid remains, roast for another 10 minutes.)
Let cool 5 minutes before serving.

GOOD TO KNOW

Leeks are remarkably amenable to different flavor pairings: add thyme or oregano to the stock before roasting, try a different type of stock (goose or duck) for a more decadent flavor, or add chili for a spicy kick.

BAKED SWEET POTATOES WITH YOGURT

Salt-baking is a popular cooking technique in new Israeli cuisine, and it is particularly appropriate for the mild taste of the sweet potato. Here, the potato's earthiness gets an additional kick from the yogurt topping, which can be mixed with whatever fresh herbs you have lying around, along with garlic and green onion for a piquant kick and a bit of crunch.

INGREDIENTS

1 lb. (500 g) coarse salt
8 medium sweet potatoes, unpeeled, washed, and dried

Dressing
½ cup (120 ml) sheep's milk yogurt
1 tbsp. chopped fresh parsley
1 tbsp. chopped green onion
1 clove garlic, minced
½ tsp. fine salt
½ tsp. freshly ground black pepper

DIRECTIONS

Preheat oven to 430°F (220°C).
Scatter half of the coarse salt evenly in a deep baking tray, place the sweet potatoes on top, and sprinkle the rest of the salt over them. Bake for 40 minutes.
Meanwhile, combine all the dressing ingredients in a small bowl and mix well.
Remove the sweet potatoes and let cool at room temperature for 15 minutes, brushing away any salt stuck to them.
Peel sweet potatoes carefully and place in a serving bowl.
Drip one tablespoon of dressing over each one and serve.

LENTILS WITH POMEGRANATE

This vegetarian dish is inspired by romanieh, an eggplant, lentil, and pomegranate mix beloved among Jaffa's Arabs. Although you will not get much color here, the lentil and pomegranate mixture is surprisingly hearty, and satisfying enough to be a full meal. Lentils are heavy enough not to need a starch accompaniment, but pair this with a chopped salad and you're good to go.

INGREDIENTS

2 tbsp. olive oil
1 onion, finely chopped
2 garlic cloves, minced
2 cups (400 g) Beluga lentils
2 cups (500 ml) vegetable stock
   (page 286)
1 cup (250 ml) pomegranate juice
3 tbsp. pomegranate
   concentrate
1 tsp. freshly ground
   black pepper
1 tbsp. salt

DIRECTIONS

Heat the olive oil in a medium saucepan, then add the onion and garlic and fry until lightly golden.
Add all other ingredients, except for the salt, and bring the mix to a boil. Reduce heat and simmer for 30 minutes, or until lentils are soft but not falling apart.
Once lentils are soft, add the salt and cook over high heat for up to 5 minutes, until the mixture thickens. Take care not to overcook the lentils, which should remain whole.

PICKLED HERRING WITH BRUSCHETTA

Salted, cured fish, beloved of Eastern European Jews, is among the few Ashkenazi dishes to find its place in new Israeli cuisine. Its pungent, fatty oiliness pairs well with alcohol, which is why you may be tempted to go for a good, stiff drink after eating one. Two would make an excellent starter; any more and you will be hooked for life. You will also be too full for dinner.

INGREDIENTS

8 slices of whole-grain
  sourdough bread, ⅓ in. (1 cm)
  thick
14 oz. (400 g) boneless pickled
  herring fillet, cut into ⅕-in.-wide
  (½-cm-wide) strips
1 red onion, thinly sliced
3 tbsp. finely chopped
  green onion
1 tbsp. apple cider vinegar
½ tsp. coarsely ground
  black pepper
1 ripe tomato, halved
4 tbsp. unsalted butter

DIRECTIONS

Toast the bread as desired in a toaster or oven.
Combine the herring, red and green onion, vinegar, and black pepper in a small bowl.
Squeeze the tomato into the bowl.
Mix carefully and make sure the fish keeps its original texture.
Spread ½ tbsp. of butter on each slice of bread, pile the herring mixture on top, and serve.

FOCACCIA WITH MIXED SEEDS

Italian-Mediterranean cuisine is one of the biggest influences on new Israeli cuisine. Focaccia, a type of traditional Italian bread, has been eagerly adopted in a region where baked flatbreads are common. Instead of adding olives and sundried tomatoes, though, Israeli chefs have gone for their own tasty interpretations, as you will see on this page and the next.

INGREDIENTS

Dough
⅓ oz. (10 g) fresh yeast
1 tbsp. honey
1½ cups (350 ml) cold water
14 oz. (400 g) white flour
4 oz. (100 g) whole-wheat flour
1 tbsp. salt
2 tbsp. extra virgin olive oil

Topping
½ cup (75 g) untoasted
   sesame seeds
½ cup (70 g) sunflower seeds
½ cup (65 g) pumpkin seeds
½ tsp. coarse salt

DIRECTIONS

Combine yeast, honey, ¾ of the amount of water, white and whole-wheat flours, and salt in the bowl of a stand mixer. Using the dough hook, knead for 3 minutes at low speed until a ball of dough forms.
Add the olive oil and knead at medium speed for another 7 minutes. While kneading, gradually add the rest of the water until it is completely absorbed.
If you do not have a stand mixer with a dough hook, knead by hand until a ball of dough forms, add the olive oil, and then knead again for 8 minutes, until the dough becomes smooth and homogenous.
Place the ball of dough in a well-greased bowl and cover with plastic wrap. Let the dough rest until double in size.
On a slightly greased work surface, divide the dough into two equal pieces. Roll out a 12×6 in. (30×15 cm) rectangle from each piece.
Line a baking tray with baking paper and place the dough rectangles on it.
Mix the topping ingredients together. Sprinkle a quarter of the topping on each rectangle, press it down into the dough, turn the dough around, and sprinkle another quarter on the other side.
When you are done, both sides of each focaccia loaf should be covered with seeds.
Let the dough rise for 1 hour.
Preheat oven to 480°F (250°C).
Bake the focaccia loaves for 20 minutes, until golden brown.
Allow to cool for 10 minutes before serving.

SWEET FOCACCIA WITH ORANGES

This delectable sweet focaccia sits in that gray area between bread and cake. Thanks to the orange liqueur and honey, it feels delightfully decadent. What is more, its unusual appearance and surprising punch of flavor seem to exist in indirect proportion to how much time you spent on it.

INGREDIENTS

Dough
3½ oz. (10 g) fresh yeast
4 tbsp. honey
1½ cups (350 ml) cold water
14 oz. (400 g) white flour
4 oz. (100 g) whole-wheat flour
1 tbsp. fine salt
3 tbsp. extra virgin olive oil

Topping
½ cup (120 ml) water
½ cup (100 g) sugar
2 oranges, cut into
    ⅕-in.-thick (½-cm-thick) slices
2 tbsp. orange liqueur
1 tbsp. thyme leaves,
    for garnishing

DIRECTIONS

Combine yeast, honey, ¾ of the amount of water, white and whole-wheat flours, and salt in the bowl of a stand mixer. Using the dough hook, knead for 3 minutes at low speed until a ball of dough forms.
Add the olive oil and knead at medium speed for another 7 minutes. While kneading, gradually add the rest of the water until it is completely absorbed.
If you do not have a stand mixer with a dough hook, knead by hand until a ball of dough forms, add the olive oil, and then knead again for 8 minutes, until the dough becomes smooth and homogenous.
Place the ball of dough in a well-greased bowl and cover with cling film. Let the dough rest until double in size.
On a slightly greased work surface, divide the dough into two equal pieces. Roll out a 30 × 15 cm (12 × 6 inch) rectangle from each piece.
Line a baking tray with baking paper and place the dough rectangles on it.
Mix the topping ingredients together. Sprinkle a quarter of the topping on each rectangle, press it down into the dough, turn the dough around, and sprinkle another quarter on the other side.
When you are done, both sides of each focaccia loaf should be covered with seeds.
Let the dough rise for 1 hour.
Preheat oven to 410°F (210°C).
Bake the focaccia loaves for 20 minutes, until golden brown.
Allow to cool for 10 minutes before serving.

CHICKEN AND ORANGE VEGETABLE SOUP

Among Ashkenazi Jews with roots in Eastern Europe, chicken soup has long been known as the "Jewish penicillin." Something about its savory saltiness, protein, and fresh vegetables seems to cure all ills. Here, an original, beloved recipe receives a colorful, modern, and delicious treatment in the form of orange-colored vegetables.

INGREDIENTS

2 carrots, peeled
7 oz. (200 g) peeled pumpkin
1 large sweet potato, peeled
1 tbsp. extra virgin olive oil
1 onion, finely chopped
4 chicken drumsticks, skinned
1 qt. (1 l) chicken stock
  (page 289)
1 tsp. fine salt

DIRECTIONS

Slice carrots into ⅕-in.-thick (½-cm-thick) slices, pumpkin into ⅓-cm (1-cm) cubes, and sweet potato into ⅘-in. (2-cm) cubes.
Heat olive oil in a medium saucepan over high heat.
Add chopped onion and fry until transparent.
Add chicken, vegetables, stock, and salt and bring to a boil.
Lower heat and simmer for 50 minutes.
Soup can be served immediately or kept refrigerated—it will taste even better the next day.

GOOD TO KNOW

Butternut squash is the best type for this soup, but any soft, slightly sweet pumpkin will do.

GROUPER-HEAD SOUP WITH LEEK KREPLACH

The texture of this soup is thick and satisfying thanks to the gelatin in the fish heads, and its taste is particularly rich. Kreplach filled with chopped leek are added to the tomato-based broth, making a satisfyingly savory and chewy addition. Just make sure to count the kreplach when serving, so no fights break out over who got more of these delicious dumplings.

INGREDIENTS

Kreplach filling
2 leeks
1 pt. (½ l) vegetable stock
   (page 286)
½ tsp. fine salt

Kreplach dough
11 oz. (300 g) white flour
¾ cup (180 ml) cold water
1 tsp. olive oil
½ tsp. fine salt

Soup
1 qt. (1 l) fish stock (page 286)
1 cup (250 ml) tomato sauce
   (page 293)
1 grouper head,
   about 1 lb. (500 g)
1 carrot, peeled
1 stalk celery, trimmed
1 tbsp. chopped fresh parsley
   leaves, for garnishing

DIRECTIONS

Chop leeks into ¾-in.-thick (2-cm-thick) slices.
Heat a small saucepan over high heat and add the leeks, vegetable stock, and salt.
Bring to a boil, then reduce heat and simmer for 1 hour, until leeks are soft.
Meanwhile, knead all dough ingredients in a bowl until a smooth, uniform dough forms.
Wrap dough in plastic wrap and refrigerate for 1 hour.
While filling is cooking and dough is refrigerating, combine all soup ingredients in a large saucepan and bring to a boil.
Reduce heat and simmer for 1 hour.
When leeks are soft, remove, drain, and let cool for 15 minutes.
With a sharp knife, chop the leeks as finely as possible on a cutting board and set aside.
After soup has cooked for 1 hour, strain, setting aside any firm pieces of fish.
Remove dough from refrigerator and roll out very thinly on a floured work surface. Cut out discs of dough, 4 in. (10 cm) in diameter.
Place a heaping teaspoon of the finely chopped leek at the center of each disc. Fold the disc in half and pinch edges to fasten.
Repeat with each disc to make as many kreplach as desired.
Add kreplach and the pieces of fish you saved to the soup and bring to a boil.
Ladle into individual serving bowls, sprinkle with chopped parsley, and serve.

SASHIMI WITH RED GRAPEFRUIT

You know of sashimi, and perhaps you have tasted ceviche. This is somewhere in between, its slices of fish as fresh and slippery as can be, the zestiness of the red grapefruit pairing well with the spice of green chili and onion. What is more, the color combination here feels fresh and clean, giving the dish a bright, playful finished look.

INGREDIENTS

14 oz. (400 g) fillets of fresh, boneless white fish
1 red grapefruit, segmented, membranes and seeds removed
½ tsp. fine salt
2 tbsp. freshly squeezed lemon juice
2 tbsp. olive oil
½ tbsp. thinly sliced fresh green Anaheim chilies, deseeded
1 tbsp. thinly sliced green onion

DIRECTIONS

Cut the fillets into 1/10-in.-thick (3-mm-thick) slices with a sharp knife, ideally a sashimi knife. Be sure to cut against the grain.
Arrange the fish slices on a serving dish, 1 in. (2–3 cm) apart, interspersed with grapefruit segments.
Sprinkle salt, lemon juice, and olive oil over the fish and grapefruit.
Garnish with the chili slices and green onion and serve.

GOOD TO KNOW

Red grapefruit makes this dish stand out, but you can also use ordinary grapefruit.

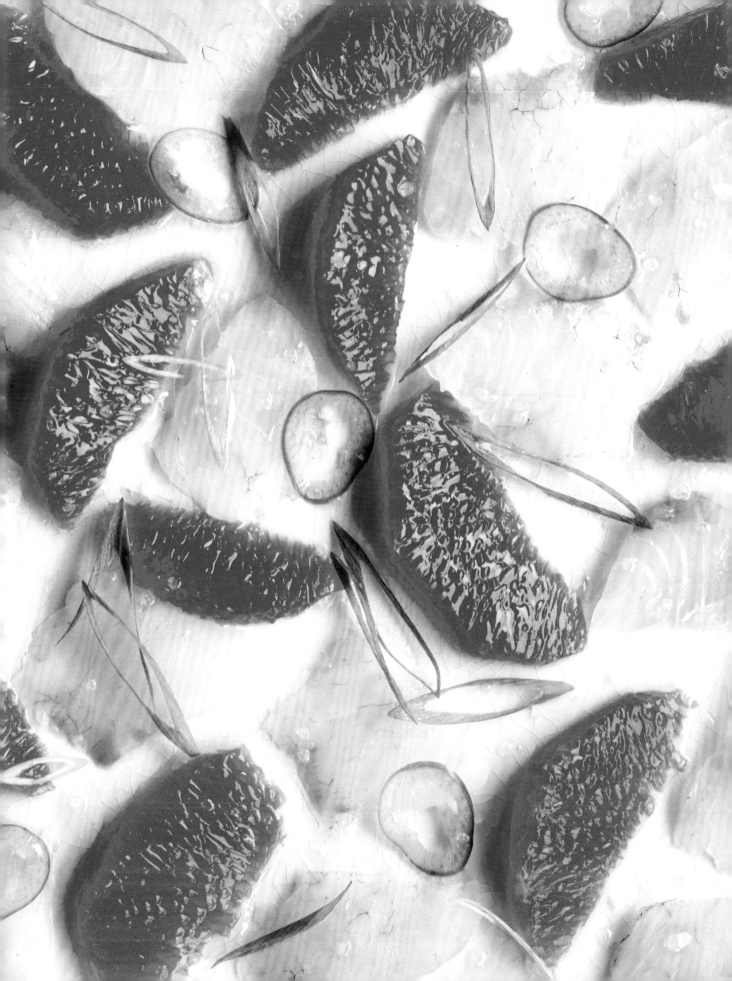

ROASTED RED MULLET

Red mullets, fried or roasted with olive oil and tomatoes and paired with a shot of arak, encapsulate the flavors of the Mediterranean. Red mullet dishes can be traced back to the free Jews of the Italian city of Livorno, who cooked them with whatever was available, or even back to ancient Rome, where this delicate, light pink fish was especially prized.

INGREDIENTS

1 cup cherry tomatoes, halved
1 leek, sliced into thin rings
4 garlic cloves, thinly sliced
4 tbsp. extra virgin olive oil
1 tsp. coarse salt
1¾ lb. (800 g) fresh red mullet, each piece weighing about ¼ lb. (100–120 g)
8 sprigs fresh thyme
1 lemon, for serving

DIRECTIONS

Preheat oven to 480°F (250°C).
Arrange tomatoes, leeks, and garlic in a flat, oven-safe skillet.
Drizzle 2 tsp. of olive oil over the vegetables and season with ½ tsp. of salt.
Roast for 12 minutes.
Place the pieces of mullet on the vegetables.
Scatter the thyme sprigs and the rest of the oil and salt on top and roast for another 8 minutes.
Squeeze the lemon over the skillet and serve immediately.

FISH BAKED IN A SALT AND HERB MANTLE

Salt- or dough-wrapped fish retains its juices and preserves its flavors particularly well. This dish was inspired by ta'ashima, a recipe from Jaffa, thought to work as a charm against unfulfilled desires that are so unbearable, they become physical ailments. This version may not grant all your wishes, but it will certainly make for a satisfying meal.

INGREDIENTS

Dough
1 lb. (500 g) white flour
2 tbsp. chopped fresh rosemary
2 tbsp. chopped fresh parsley
2 tbsp. fresh thyme leaves
2 tbsp. finely chopped
   green onion
7 oz. (200 g) coarse salt
3 eggs
¾ cup (180 ml) cold water
2 tbsp. olive oil

2 sea bream, whole, gutted
   and scaled, 1½ – 1¾ lb.
   (700 – 800 g) each
½ lemon, cut into ⅕-in.-thick
   (½-cm-thick) slices
½ tsp. freshly ground
   black pepper

DIRECTIONS

Combine dough ingredients in the bowl of a stand mixer, and knead on low speed with the dough hook until the dough is green and uniform. If you do not have a stand mixer, you can also knead by hand until the dough is green and uniform.
Wrap dough in plastic wrap and refrigerate for half an hour.
Preheat the oven to 480°F (250°C).
Divide the dough into 2 equal balls on a floured work surface.
Roll out each dough ball into a ⅕-in.-thick (4-mm-thick) disc.
Place a fish in the center of each disc.
Cut along the abdomen of the fish with a sharp knife to open it up.
Arrange lemon inside the cavity of each fish and season with black pepper.
Wrap fish entirely with the dough and pinch the edges to seal.
Place both fish "packages" on a baking pan and bake for 30 minutes.
Cut each fish "package" open slightly to reveal the fish inside, making it easier to eat, then serve.

CRAB AND BULGUR RISOTTO

A Middle Eastern take on Italian risotto, in which light, fluffy bulgur replaces the heavier, more glutinous rice. The juices of the crab mix with the fish stock to add a pleasing pungency, and the turmeric (use fresh if you can find it) lends the dish an even brighter color and flavor. This dish would also work well with couscous or quinoa, topped with fresh herbs.

INGREDIENTS

2 tbsp. extra virgin olive oil
2 garlic cloves, minced
8 fresh crabs, shells removed and cleaned
½ tsp. ground turmeric
½ tsp. sweet paprika
2 tsp. coarse salt
2½ cups (600 ml) fish stock (page 286)
¼ cup (60 ml) tomato sauce (page 293)
14 oz. (400 g) coarse bulgur

DIRECTIONS

Heat the olive oil in a wide saucepan. Add the garlic and fry until lightly golden.
Add the crabs, turmeric, paprika, and salt and stir well.
Pour in the fish stock and tomato sauce, stir, and bring to a boil.
Reduce the heat and add the bulgur.
Simmer over low heat for 15–20 minutes, stirring occasionally, until the bulgur is soft and has absorbed the liquid.
Place in a serving dish and serve immediately.

SEAFOOD PAN ROAST

Almost every Mediterranean country has its own anise-based drink and its own favorite dishes to drink it with. Across Israel, in the region once called Greater Syria, it is arak. The classic combination of anise and seafood is particularly popular in local restaurants, and local arak can be replaced with Pernod, pastis, ouzo, or any other anise-based drink.

INGREDIENTS

2 tbsp. olive oil
½ tsp. finely chopped fresh
   red Anaheim chilies, deseeded
2 garlic cloves, minced
1 tbsp. finely chopped
   preserved lemons (page 294)
12 large shrimp, tails on
6 fresh crabs, shells removed
   and cleaned
11 oz. (300 g) calamari, cleaned
   and cut into ⅘-in.-thick
   (2-cm-thick) rings
2 tbsp. Pernod, arak, or similar
½ cup (60 ml) fish stock
   (page 286)
1 tsp. fine salt

DIRECTIONS

Heat the olive oil in a wide pan, then add chili and garlic and sauté until lightly golden.
Add preserved lemons and stir well.
Add shrimp, crabs, and calamari and splash the Pernod on top.
Pour in fish stock, add salt, and cook covered for 5 minutes over high heat.
Remove pan from heat and let cool 5 minutes, covered, before serving.

GOOD TO KNOW

Yes, you can always use normal sliced lemons to replace preserved lemons, but try the dish with preserved lemons at least once. You'll notice quite a difference in flavor.

STEAMED SHRIMP DUMPLINGS

Israel has no large Asian community, but it does harbor a love for Asian cuisine. In recent years Asian influences have crept into local cuisines, inspiring new generations of chefs eager to prove themselves to an increasingly international audience. Do not let dumplings intimidate you—they may be time-consuming, but they are really rather easy to make.

INGREDIENTS

Dough
11 oz. (300 g) white flour
3 eggs
½ tsp. fine salt
1 tbsp. olive oil

Filling
11 oz. (300 g) peeled shrimp
1 tbsp. chopped fresh parsley
1 tbsp. chopped shallots
2 tbsp. olive oil
½ tsp. fine salt
½ tsp. freshly ground
  black pepper

1½ qt. (1½ l) fish stock (page 286)
A few drops of lemon juice

DIRECTIONS

Place dough ingredients in the bowl of a stand mixer and knead with the dough hook until a ball of dough forms. If you do not have a stand mixer, knead by hand until a ball of dough forms.
Wrap dough ball in plastic wrap, and refrigerate for 40 minutes.
Meanwhile, chop the shrimp with a heavy knife, place in a bowl with the rest of the filling ingredients, and mix well until mixture is uniform. Refrigerate mixture until cool.
Roll out the dough very thinly on a floured work surface. If you are using a pasta maker, adjust to setting 6.
Cut discs out of the dough 4 in. (10 cm) in diameter.
Place a tablespoon of the filling in each disc. Fold the edges upwards and pinch together to create a flower shape.
Bring fish stock to a boil in a large saucepan. Place a steamer on top of the pan and arrange dumplings inside. Cover and steam the dumplings for 7–8 minutes.
Place steamer on a wide plate, squeeze a few drops of lemon on top, and serve.

GOOD TO KNOW

If you do not have a round cookie-cutter, the round opening of an over-turned cup or glass will work just as well for cutting out small discs.
If you do not have a steamer, a wire mesh sieve with a flat bottom will do.

SLOW-ROASTED BEEF BRISKET

This is a local take on the renowned Ashkenazi brisket, a dish that Jews remember fondly when served at family Shabbat dinners, Seders, or as leftovers inside two pieces of bread. Used in many types of barbecue and in the making of the beloved New York pastrami, brisket has won appreciation in metropolises worldwide—anywhere Jews live and thrive.

INGREDIENTS

4½ lb. (2 kg) beef brisket,
  cut from the thickest section
½ cup (60 ml) pomegranate
  concentrate
1 tbsp. coarse salt
3 tbsp. freshly ground
  black pepper
4 tbsp. fine mustard, to serve

DIRECTIONS

Preheat oven to 285°F (140°C).
Brush brisket with pomegranate concentrate and season with salt and pepper on all sides.
Place brisket in a heavy, oven-safe casserole or cast-iron pot.
Cover and roast for 8 hours.
Let cool for 1 hour, still covered.
Carefully remove the brisket.
On a cutting board, cut the brisket into ⅓-in.-thick (1-cm-thick) slices using a serrated knife.
Serve with fine mustard.

LAMB SPARE RIBS WITH CITRUS MARINADE

Lamb and lemons are a familiar combination, but here the lemons are replaced by oranges and the results are surprisingly delicious. The two ingredients essentially swap flavors, with the oranges softening up nicely as they roast, absorbing some of the juices of the lamb, while the orange juice provides a sweet and acidic glaze for the lamb.

INGREDIENTS

Marinade
Juice of 1 orange
1 tbsp. orange zest
3 garlic cloves, minced
1 tbsp. thyme leaves
1 tbsp. olive oil
1 tbsp. honey
1 tsp. coarse salt
1 tsp. freshly ground
   black pepper
½ tsp. finely chopped fresh
   green chili pepper, deseeded

2 lb. (1 kg) lamb spare ribs,
   separated

DIRECTIONS

Preheat oven to 390°F (200°C).
Combine all the marinade ingredients in a bowl and mix well.
Arrange the spare ribs in a deep roasting tray.
Pour the marinade over the meat and cover with a double layer of aluminum foil.
Roast for 1 hour.
Remove aluminum foil and roast, uncovered, for another 15–20 minutes, until ribs are golden brown.
Serve hot.

ROASTED SHOULDER OF LAMB

A celebratory dish in many cultures, this roasted lamb shoulder is paired simply and successfully with Mediterranean herbs. The roulade, a meat roll enjoyed by Ashkenazi Jews all over Europe, keeps the meat succulent and the flavors concentrated. It also has the added benefit of looking particularly impressive when presented hot and sliced on the table.

INGREDIENTS

1 boneless shoulder of lamb,
3½–4 lb. (1.6–1.8 kg)

1 tbsp. chopped fresh
mint leaves

1 tsp. chopped rosemary

3 garlic cloves, minced

2 tbsp. olive oil,
plus more for roasting

½ tsp. coarse salt,
plus more for roasting

1 tsp. freshly ground
black pepper,
plus more for roasting

½ tsp. lemon zest

2 sprigs of rosemary

DIRECTIONS

Preheat oven to 480°F (250°C).

Place shoulder of lamb with the fat side up on a cutting board.

Rub mint, rosemary, garlic, olive oil, salt, pepper, and lemon zest into the lamb.

Roll meat into a roulade and tie it tightly with kitchen twine, placing the rosemary sprigs between the knots.

Brush the roulade with a tablespoon of olive oil and season with salt and pepper on all sides.

Roast for 10 minutes. Lower the oven temperature to 390°F (200°C) and roast for another 20 minutes.

Remove roulade from the oven, wrap with aluminum foil and let cool for 20 minutes.

On a cutting board, remove the foil and kitchen twine.

Cut the roast into 1/10-in.-thick (3–4-mm-thick) slices and serve hot.

DRIED FRUIT CAKE

Preserved dried fruit has always been an important component of the diets of those living in arid regions where it is difficult to grow fruit in the first place and there are no means of cooling food. Meanwhile, practically every Western culture has its fruit cake. Almonds, pistachios, dates, and figs make this one unforgettable, as well as a particularly splendid accompaniment to coffee.

INGREDIENTS

4 eggs
6 oz. (170 g) sugar
7 oz. (200 g) unsalted butter, melted
7 oz. (200 g) ground almonds
6 oz. (150 g) Medjool dates, coarsely chopped
6 oz. (150 g) dried figs, cut into ⅕-in.-wide (½-cm-wide) strips
4 oz. (100 g) whole pistachios, peeled
5 drops almond extract

DIRECTIONS

Preheat oven to 340°F (170°C).
Place eggs and sugar in the bowl of a stand mixer and beat until mixture is pale and foamy. Alternatively, place eggs and sugar in a tall-sided bowl and beat with a hand-held mixer.
While beating, slowly pour the melted butter into the bowl until it is fully incorporated. Gradually add the ground almonds until fully incorporated. Add dates, figs, pistachios, and almond extract and fold into the mixture using a spatula.
Pour the mixture into an oiled baking tin and smooth the surface evenly with a spatula.
Place the tin in the oven and bake for 50 minutes, until cake is dark brown. Allow to cool before serving.
The cake can be kept for up to 3 days in an airtight container.

GOOD TO KNOW

You can bake this in a 10-in. (26-cm) round baking tin or springform pan. If you are using the springform, you can simply place a square of baking paper at the bottom of the springform and then clamp the round sprung collar down over it.

PISTACHIO CAKE

A moist, versatile dessert that is easy to make but still pretty enough to serve as an appropriate ending to a feast, this cake is part of a Middle Eastern tradition. It combines the nutty flavor of pistachios with the zesty freshness of lemon glaze, but could work just as well with a dash of rosewater or with candied oranges in syrup instead of lemon glaze.

INGREDIENTS

5 medium eggs
4¼ oz. (120 g) sugar
7 oz. (200 g) unsalted butter, melted
1¾ oz. (50 g) white flour
½ tsp. baking powder
7 oz. (200 g) ground pistachios
½ tsp. lemon zest
4 drops almond extract

Frosting
3½ oz. (100 g) powdered sugar
1 tbsp. freshly squeezed lemon juice

DIRECTIONS

Preheat oven to 340°F (170°C).
Line the bottom of a baking pan with a circle of baking paper, 10 in. (26 cm) in diameter.
In a stand mixer, whip the eggs at high speed until foamy. Alternatively, beat the eggs in a tall-sided bowl with a hand-held mixer.
Continue whipping, gradually adding the sugar until fully incorporated. Add the melted butter gradually.
Put the mixer on low speed and add the flour, baking powder, pistachios, lemon zest, and almond extract.
Pour the mixture into the pan and bake for 35 minutes.
Remove the cake from the oven, cover with a clean dishtowel and let cool for 40 minutes.
Invert the cake onto a serving dish and carefully remove the baking paper.
Mix powdered sugar and lemon juice in a small bowl until mixture is white, smooth, and uniform. Pour over the cake and allow to cool.
Cake can be served immediately or stored for up to 3 days in an airtight container.

GOOD TO KNOW

You can bake this in a 10-in. (26-cm) round baking tin or springform pan. If you are using the springform, you can simply place a square of baking paper at the bottom of the springform and then clamp the round sprung collar down over it.

CHOCOLATE AND HALVA ROLL

The Arabic word halva refers to various sweetmeats. In Hebrew it connotes a sweet made of ground sesame seeds (tahini) and sugar syrup (replacing honey in the ancient world). Halva can be eaten as is, or added to other pastries and desserts, from cakes and cookies to ice cream and mousse. Combining halva and chocolate is a modern invention, now popular in Israel.

INGREDIENTS

Dough
10 ½ oz. (300 g) white flour
7 oz. (200 g) unsalted butter
½ cup (60 ml) powdered sugar
½ tsp. salt
1 egg
½ tsp. baking powder

Filling
7 oz. (200 g) dark chocolate
2 oz. (60 g) unsalted butter
5 oz. (150 g) halva, crumbled
(page 296)

DIRECTIONS

Place dough ingredients in a food processor and pulse until a uniform ball of dough forms. Alternatively, use a pastry cutter to evenly distribute the butter, then form into a ball by hand.
Wrap dough ball with plastic wrap and refrigerate for 30 minutes.
Melt the chocolate and butter in a bain-marie while stirring, until the mixture is smooth and uniform.
Remove it from the heat and let cool to room temperature.
Once cooled, place in the freezer for 5 minutes.
Preheat oven to 355°F (180°C).
Roll the dough into a 20 × 10 in. (50 × 30 cm) rectangle on a floured work surface.
Spread the chocolate mixture over the dough and sprinkle the halva on top.
Line a baking tray with baking paper.
Roll the dough into a roulade and press together well.
Slice the roulade into 12 equally thick slices and place on a baking tray. Each slice should have a perfect spiral of dough and filling, like a cinnamon roll.
Bake 20 minutes, until slices are golden-brown.
Let cool 20 minutes before serving.

GOOD TO KNOW

To approximate a bain-marie or "water bath," place a heat-proof saucepan inside a larger pan of boiling water.

RICE PUDDING

Rice pudding is a Jewish specialty of Turkey and the Balkans, as well as a delicious dessert beloved the world over.
The mild, milky sweetness of the rice goes particularly well with homemade quince or apricot jam. You can also make rice pudding as part of a sweet breakfast, using it as a base for various nut and seed toppings, almost like oatmeal.

INGREDIENTS

1 pt. (½ l) full-fat milk
2 tbsp. sugar
1 tsp. cinnamon
½ tsp. orange zest
1 cup (120 g) rice flour
2 tbsp. unsalted butter

DIRECTIONS

Combine milk, sugar, cinnamon, and orange zest in a small saucepan and bring to a boil.
Reduce the heat and add rice flour gradually, while stirring.
Cook over low heat, stirring constantly, for 10 minutes.
Add butter, stir well, and remove from heat.
Cover and let sit for ten minutes.
Stir well and serve.

JERUSALEM

Jerusalem means many things to many people. With millennia of history in its walls, Jerusalem is also a melting pot as far as food is concerned. Pilgrims of different eras brought their culinary traditions with them, and these have turned into universally beloved dishes. Bagels and challah, hummus and shawarma, kubbeh and kugel—everyone claims them as their own, and, just like Jerusalem itself, they belong to everybody.

AT THE HEART OF THE WORLD

Straddling the dividing line between Israel and the West Bank, its borders redrawn multiple times in the twentieth century, Jerusalem has always been a point of convergence and contention among the world's three major religions—Judaism, Islam, and Christianity. Its food, too, seems to have been taken from all over the world, yet many of its products come from small farmers, growers, and butchers who live in the immediate vicinity and travel to Jerusalem with their wares on market days.

Today, every piece of Jerusalem's culinary mosaic still exists side by side. It is a melting pot generating dishes with distinctly local characteristics.

Above: **Jerusalem bakers are either staunch adherents of ancient techniques or, like baker Russell Sacks, proud champions of the new guard.** Below: **Nasser Abu Senana baking bagels at his family bakery in East Jerusalem.**

A million things to millions of people over millennia, Jerusalem by all rights should be a terrific letdown by the time you finally set foot there. Yet somehow, it not only lives up to expectations but exceeds them, perhaps best evidenced by the phenomenon of Jerusalem syndrome, when visitors become so enamored of the ancient city, they actually imagine themselves to be a sacred figure like the Messiah or to have traveled back in time to the Biblical era. A holy pilgrimage site to the world's three major religions, a meeting place of ancient and modern history and cultures, Jerusalem is not just a city but an experience. Jerusalem has inspired peace, sacrifice, and devotion, sparked wars, and caused madness. Wandering around Jerusalem's sand-colored, labyrinthine walls, alleyways, and souks (markets), with the gold-topped Dome of the Rock in the background, it is easy to see why. Scholars of Jerusalem maintain that the city's history is in fact the history

Rows of puffed, chewy pita ready to be filled with falafel, vegetables, hummus, or lamb to make lamb shawarma (page 202).

A holy pilgrimage site to the world's
three major religions, as well as a
meeting place of ancient and modern
history and cultures, Jerusalem
is not just a city but an experience.

Machneyuda is a modern market restaurant offering a menu based on raw ingredients for sale in the nearby Mahaneh Yehuda market.

Just about every Middle Eastern culture has claimed hummus as its own. Rich or poor, Jewish or Muslim—every one scoops up hummus with pita bread, and every-one argues about who makes it best.

The market is a place to eat as much as a place to shop. Chef Pini Levi, of the Kosher restaurant Pini's Kitchen sharpens his knife in preparation for carving up meat (left) that will go onto skewers (below).

of the world, so it can get more than a bit overwhelming to contemplate all those years of human achievement directly under your feet.

Of course, all those millions of visitors over thousands of years had to eat something. Pilgrims to the Holy City brought with them not only their languages and cultures, but their diverse cooking traditions and dining customs as well. Leaders of armies and their troops, traders, and administrators who passed through Jerusalem in its glory days, missionaries and pilgrims who faithfully returned to it even in eras of decline—all have left their traces on the city's culinary landscape.

Today, every piece of that culinary mosaic still exists side by side, though the melting pot of Jerusalem has generated dishes with distinctly local characteristics. Like many Israeli dishes, those truly labeled "Jerusalemite" have a

Traditional dishes are cooked in large saucepans on kerosene stoves at Kurdish greasy-spoon restaurants like this one in the Mahaneh Yehuda market.

Jerusalem's welcoming, hole-in-the-wall restaurants, such as Máchneyuda in the city's Mahaneh Yehuda market, can feel more like cosy living rooms than professional establishments.

WHAT IS KOSHER?

There are a few commonly known rules of kosher—no pork, no seafood, and meat and dairy must be kept separate. But of course, kosher law is far more complex than that. Animals must be slaughtered according to certain rules and rituals, and only by a certain type of rabbi (similar rules apply in the Muslim slaughtering practice known as halal). All kosher foods must be certified as such by a rabbi or organization of rabbis. What's more, no work can be done on the Sabbath, and that is where the dish known as hamin comes in (like Macaroni Hamin, page 210). This dish can be assembled before sundown on Friday and then cooked overnight, ready to be eaten on Saturday.

long history behind them, a long list of predecessors born across multiple borders. They include dishes like hummus, made of crushed chickpeas and tahini, which just about every Middle Eastern culture has claimed as its own. Rich or poor, Jewish or Arab, in East or West Jerusalem—everyone scoops up hummus with pita bread, and everyone argues about who makes the definitive version.

Jerusalem's markets are places where old meets new and locals of very different backgrounds come together over the most important topic of daily life: food. The Old City's market is one of East Jerusalem's focal points. Its genesis dates back to the Roman-Byzantine period 2,000 years ago. During the Crusades, pilgrims used to call it "the market of foul odors," in reference to the cooking smells wafting through—though perhaps the odors were not so much foul as simply foreign to them. Today's market was built during the Ottoman rule and modeled after Istanbul's Grand Bazaar. Its alleys are still just wide enough to let donkeys pass through. Here is where you will find baladi (local varieties) of vegetables and fruits, tahini and halva produced in dozens of small presses in Nablus, the region's tahini capital, and fresh coffee from family-owned roasteries. There is lamb from the butchers' alley, spice shops showcasing heaps of za'atar spice mix, and modest restaurants serving hummus, charcoal-grilled kebab skewers, and traditional dishes like kofta (meatballs) and maqluba (an upside-down rice and meat casserole).

The open-air Mahaneh Yehuda market, in contrast, came about in the late nineteenth century, constructed outside the walls of the Old City on the West Jerusalem side. Fruit and vegetable stands line its alleys, and there are delis selling local cheeses, pickled fish, and slices of Jerusalem kugel, an Ashkenazi dish of caramelized noodle, traditionally baked overnight ahead of the Sabbath. Century-old bakeries line their shelves with challah, the bread eaten on the Sabbath and Jewish holidays, while just next door, young bakers turn out focaccia bread and French breakfast pastries in modern establishments.

This page: **Loaves of challah, one of Judaism's seminal recipes, ready for sale at the Landner bakery in Jerusalem's Beit Israel ultra-orthodox neighborhood.** Opposite page: Roasting sesame seeds at a tahini factory in East Jerusalem.

Century-old bakeries line their shelves with challah, the bread eaten on the Sabbath and Jewish holidays.

Nearby, hole-in-the-wall restaurants specialize in grilled offal, and Jewish Kurdish eateries simmer heritage dishes over kerosene stoves. Just about every menu offers something stuffed: a stuffed fruit or vegetable, stuffed pastries like baklava, stuffed neck of lamb, or the stuffed semolina dumplings known as kubbeh. Muslim, Christian, and Jewish homes all churn out countless variations of stuffed foods—a beloved but labor-intensive form of cooking that used to be reserved only for holiday meals but has now received widespread attention.

The Jerusalem bagel (ka'ak in Arabic) is also enjoyed by nearly all city residents, regardless of creed or class. An elongated ring of dough sprinkled with toasted sesame seeds, it is baked in traditional wooden stoves in family-owned bakeries in the Old City's Muslim quarter. A Jewish influence—sour cream—has been added to it to make part of East Jerusalem's most popular breakfast: a bagel served with za'atar, falafel, and a hard-boiled egg. Although the modern-day bagel only bears a passing resemblance to Jerusalem's sesame-covered rings, it has nevertheless been one of the seeds of a mainstream phenomenon: the near global obsession with bagels.

Meanwhile, outside the city walls, nature does its part to contribute to the flavors of old Jerusalem. Wild caper bushes flourish in the walls' crevices, and the hills around the city are home to wild herbs consumed since Biblical times. These herbs were once an important source of nutrition for people who could

INTRODUCING...
THE BAGEL

The debate rages on about the origins of this globally beloved snack. Was the bagel first seen in Ancient Rome or Ancient Egypt? Does it have roots in Eastern Europe or in the Middle East? The bagel may have started life in Poland, brought over to the New World by Yiddish-speaking Jews (beigel, anyone?), but today it is most closely associated with New York City, where it is rumored that the water gives it its classic dense, chewy texture and glossy crust. Montreal and London have both claimed their own bagel types, and in this chapter you will learn how to make the elongated, sesame-crusted Jerusalem bagel.

Old meets new at Jerusalem's markets, and locals of very different backgrounds come together over the most important topic of daily life: food.

not grow their own vegetables. Today, Arab and Jewish women still go out to the fields to collect purslane, nettles, ox-tongue, mallow, and Jerusalem sage. Local herbs are sold in markets in both halves of the city, and over the years have made their way from local kitchens to the city's top restaurants, run by chefs eager to pay homage to their city's many past lives.

Of course, Jerusalem's history is far from over. There is no longer a border running directly through the city center, but a bitterly conflicted political reality still creates an intangible chasm between Jerusalem's two halves, a daily reminder of the strife that still marks the entire region. Two twentieth-century wars—the Arab-Israeli War of 1948 and the Six-Day War of 1967—redrew Jerusalem's borders, defining anew who could settle where, who could work in which half of the city, and indeed, to whom Jerusalem even truly belongs. The answer, of course, is no one. And everyone. Beautiful yet complex, fragile yet everlasting, a city that evokes such powerful images in those who admire it and those who would seek to conquer it, Jerusalem is truly a place outside of time. May we all catch a glimpse of it—and a taste of it—in our lifetimes.

Opposite page: Abu
Hassan el Baghdadi
prepares herbs and
vegetables at Sultani
Restaurant in East
Jerusalem, considered
to be one of the
best humus and ke-
bab restaurants in
the city. This page:
The ovens at Mati
Landner's third-
generation Challah
bakery were built
by a blacksmith in
the 19th century.

ROOTED IN TRADITION

Recipes from Jerusalem rely on a lot of root vegetables, lamb, and tomato sauces. Dishes often require long roasting or baking times, but the result is outstanding texture and flavor. Stuffed dishes mingle hardy vegetables with aromatic meats and grains, while herbs that grow wild in the mountains surrounding the city make an appearance in casseroles, soups, and even the humble omelet.

Masabeha, a variation of hummus in which whole chickpeas are mixed with lemon-spiked tahini and garnished liberally with paprika.

ROASTED CAULIFLOWER AND CHICKPEA SALAD

Cauliflower is one of those beautiful ingredients utterly transformed by heat. Raw it is nothing special; once roasted in the oven its flavor mellows, its florets crisp up, and it achieves something close to perfection. Fried or roasted cauliflower with tahini is common in Palestinian cuisine, here joined by cooked chickpeas with their earthy flavor and soft texture.

INGREDIENTS

½ cup (100 g) dried chickpeas
1 tsp. baking soda
2 tsp. coarse salt
2 small heads of cauliflower
4 tbsp. extra virgin olive oil,
   plus more for serving
¼ tsp. fine salt
⅓ cup (80 ml) raw tahini paste
½ cup (120 ml) cold water
Juice of ½ lemon

DIRECTIONS

One day in advance:
Thoroughly wash the chickpeas, place them in a large bowl,
cover with water, and add the baking soda. Leave to soak overnight.

Day of:
Drain the chickpeas, place in a saucepan, and add water to cover.
Bring to a boil on high heat, then reduce the heat and let simmer for
1½ hours, or until chickpeas are very soft. Set aside.
Fill another saucepan with water, add the coarse salt, and bring to a boil.
Add the heads of cauliflower and cook over high heat for 8 minutes.
Preheat oven to 480°F (250°C).
Line a roasting tray with greaseproof paper. Remove the cauliflowers
with a slotted spoon and place on the prepared tray. Pour the olive oil
over them and sprinkle with fine salt.
Roast for 25 minutes, or until parts of the cauliflower have turned
golden brown.
In a small bowl, mix the raw tahini paste, water, lemon juice, and fine salt
until smooth.
Remove cauliflowers from the oven, cut into ¾-in.-thick (2-cm-thick) slices,
and place in a bowl.
Gently mix together drained chickpeas, roasted cauliflower slices,
and half the tahini sauce, and arrange in a serving bowl.
Pour the rest of the tahini on top, add a tablespoon of olive oil, and serve.

BABY ZUCCHINI AND LABANEH SALAD

The power of this recipe lies in its simplicity, and in the taste of the fine ingredients. Baby zucchini, with their attractive appearance and delicate flavor, are cooked whole and served with balls of labaneh preserved in olive oil for a simple meze that pairs well with many other salad or vegetable dishes. Good bread for mopping up the oil at the end is a must.

INGREDIENTS

2 tbsp. coarse sea salt
12 whole baby zucchini
4 tbsp. olive oil
¼ tsp. fine salt
10 labaneh balls, stored in
    olive oil (page 42)

DIRECTIONS

Fill a medium saucepan with 1½ l (1½ qt.) of water, add the salt, and place over high heat. Once the water begins to boil, reduce the heat. Add the zucchini to the water and place a sheet of greaseproof paper on top of the water, to keep them from floating to the top (you can skip this step, but the zucchini will be especially crisp for it).
Cook for 35 minutes or until zucchini are cooked through but still firm. Carefully remove zucchini with a slotted spoon and cool on a plate for 15 minutes.
Dip each zucchini into a little olive oil, sprinkle with fine salt, then, taking care not to use too much pressure, gently massage in until the zucchini's skin is slightly bruised.
Place zucchini in a serving bowl with labaneh balls in between, drizzle with olive oil, and serve.

HERB OMELET

Every culture has its omelet, and this one incorporates the fresh herbs sold in Jerusalem's markets or even found growing wild outside the city walls. Served with tahini and fresh tomato slices, the herb omelet is a popular breakfast in Jerusalem. Packed in a pita or a soft white-bread sandwich, it also becomes a wonderfully versatile, no-mess street snack.

INGREDIENTS

1 cup (150 g) spinach leaves, washed and chopped into thin strips

1 cup (150 g) swiss chard, washed and chopped into thin strips

1 cup (150 g) chopped fresh herbs according to preference (parsley, coriander, green onion, basil, mint, dill, or tarragon)

1 small onion, finely chopped

2 garlic cloves, minced

4 eggs, beaten

1 pinch salt

1 pinch freshly ground black pepper

Extra virgin olive oil, for frying

DIRECTIONS

Combine all ingredients except for the olive oil in a medium bowl.
In a non-stick frying pan, heat the oil over medium-high heat.
Pour the mixture evenly into the frying pan and fry until golden on both sides.
Season with salt and pepper and serve.

JERUSALEM ARTICHOKE SOUP

This knobbly tuber is not actually an artichoke, nor does it hail from Jerusalem. Alternatively called a sunchoke, girasole artichoke, or topinambur in different parts of the world, the Jerusalem artichoke has a mild, nutty, earthy flavor that turns sweet when cooked, and adapts well to many different dishes. All this has made it a favorite in Jerusalem.

INGREDIENTS

2 tbsp. unsalted butter

1 onion, finely chopped

1¾ lb. (800 g) Jerusalem
   artichokes, peeled and cut
   into ⅕-in. (½-cm) chunks

1 qt. (1 l) of chicken (page 289)
   or vegetable stock (page 286)

1 tbsp. fresh za'atar
   or oregano leaves

2 tsp. salt

½ tsp. freshly ground
   white pepper

DIRECTIONS

Heat butter in a medium saucepan over high heat. Add the onion and cook until soft and slightly golden.

Add the rest of the ingredients and bring to a boil. Reduce heat to low and simmer, covered, for 50 minutes, until Jerusalem artichoke chunks are quite soft and falling into the soup slightly.

Season with salt and pepper to taste, and serve.

SWISS CHARD AND MEATBALL SOUP

Kubbeh—stuffed semolina dumplings—are the Jewish Kurdish community's contribution to Jerusalem's soups. In West Jerusalem, hole-in-the-wall restaurants still cook kubbeh soups on kerosene stoves; beetroot kubbeh is arguably the most renowned. This recipe preserves the flavors of this distinctive Jerusalem dish but replaces the dumplings with meatballs.

INGREDIENTS

Soup
1 large beetroot, peeled
2 cups (70 g) Swiss chard leaves, washed and dried
2 tbsp. extra virgin olive oil
1 onion, finely chopped
2 garlic cloves, minced
½ tsp. finely chopped fresh green Anaheim chili, deseeded
1 cup (250 ml) canned, crushed tomatoes
1 qt. (1 l) chicken or beef stock (page 289)
2 tsp. coarse salt

Meatballs
1⅓ lb. (600 g) minced beef
1 tsp. fine salt
1 egg
1 tsp. sweet paprika
⅓ cup (10 g) finely chopped fresh parsley
3 slices of day-old bread, crust removed, soaked in cold water and squeezed dry

DIRECTIONS

Grate beetroot on a coarse grater and cut chard leaves into ⅓-in. (1-cm) strips.
Heat olive oil over medium heat in a large saucepan.
Sauté the onion, garlic, and chili until mixture is slightly golden.
Add crushed tomatoes and bring to a boil.
Add stock, grated beetroot, and salt and bring to a boil again.
Add chard leaves, then reduce heat and cook over low heat for 1 hour.
Meanwhile, place all meatball ingredients except the bread in a large bowl.
Crumble the bread into the bowl and mix until the texture resembles soft dough.
Lightly oil your hands, then roll the mixture into 12 balls.
Add the meatballs to the simmering soup, continue cooking over low heat for another 20 minutes until meatballs are cooked through, then serve.

OKRA IN TOMATO SAUCE

Beloved among chefs in Africa and the southern United States, okra is one of those underrepresented vegetables that never quite gets its due. Regularly served in both Arab and Jewish restaurants, this dish envelops the earthy funk of okra pods in a rich tomato sauce, and adds a dash of heat as well. Be sure to use plenty of fluffy bread to mop up the sauce afterwards.

INGREDIENTS

3 tbsp. extra virgin olive oil
3 garlic cloves, minced
1 red Anaheim chili, roughly chopped
½ lb. (230 g) plum tomatoes, halved
½ lb. (230 g) ripe red vine tomatoes, quartered
Fresh basil leaves, from 2 sprigs
Salt and pepper to taste
1 lb. (450 g) fresh okra, preferably the long variety

DIRECTIONS

Lightly sauté olive oil, garlic, and chili in a medium, heavy-based saucepan over high heat.
Add both kinds of tomatoes, basil, salt, and pepper, then cook, stirring occasionally.
Once the mixture comes to a boil, reduce heat and simmer for 10–12 minutes until the tomatoes soften and release their juices.
Remove from heat and pass the contents through a coarse sieve placed over a bowl. Use a wooden spoon to press the tomatoes and basil well, extracting all their liquid.
Transfer the sauce to a clean saucepan, then simmer over low heat.
Meanwhile, in another large saucepan, bring 1½ qt. (1½ l) of water to a boil with 3 tbsp. salt (do not skimp on the salt—the water must be salty).
Add the okra and let cook for 5–6 minutes, until still firm yet slightly soft on the outside.
Drain okra, add to the saucepan with the tomato sauce, and stir well.
Cook over low heat for 20 minutes, stirring occasionally, then serve.

ROASTED CARROTS WITH POMEGRANATE AND CITRUS SAUCE

A modern take on Ashkenazi tzimmes, a traditional stew made of root vegetables and dried fruit, this dish tones down the sweetness, using just a bit of pomegranate and orange in place of the original's prunes and raisins. Though you can make this dish using just orange carrots, try to find a full range of different colors for a really stunning presentation.

INGREDIENTS

3 orange carrots, peeled
3 white carrots, peeled
3 yellow carrots, peeled
3 black carrots, peeled
2 tbsp. extra virgin olive oil
½ tsp. coarse salt

Sauce
2 tbsp. pomegranate
   concentrate
2 tbsp. extra virgin olive oil
1 tbsp. freshly squeezed
   lemon juice
1 tbsp. thyme leaves
½ tsp. orange zest
2 garlic cloves, finely chopped
½ tsp. coarse salt
½ tsp. freshly ground
   black pepper

DIRECTIONS

Preheat oven to 480°F (250°C), and line a roasting tray with baking paper.
Arrange carrots on the tray, drizzle with olive oil and sprinkle the salt on top.
Roast for 15 minutes.
Meanwhile, combine sauce ingredients in a bowl and mix well
until smooth and uniform.
Pour half the sauce over the carrots, shake the tray once or twice,
and roast for another 6 minutes.
Arrange carrots on a serving dish and pour the rest of the sauce on top.
Let cool for 15 minutes before serving.

JERUSALEM-STYLE BAGELS

Examples of ring-shaped pastries can be found all over the world, but the elongated Jerusalem bagel (ka'ak in Arabic) has become a city symbol. In the alleys of the Old City these bagels are sold by street merchants and eaten with a za'atar spice mix (see page 290). They make a common breakfast in East Jerusalem paired with za'atar, warm falafel, and hard-boiled eggs.

INGREDIENTS

1½ cups (350 ml) water
¼ cup (50 g) sugar
1 lb. (500 g) white flour
2⅓ tbsp. extra virgin olive oil
1 heaping tsp. fine salt
¾ oz. (25 g) fresh yeast

Glaze
½ tsp. baking soda
½ cup (120 ml) lukewarm water
5 oz. (150 g) sesame seeds

DIRECTIONS

Place 1 cup (250 ml) water, sugar, flour, 2 tbsp. olive oil, salt, and yeast in bowl of stand mixer. Knead with dough hook for 3 minutes at low speed. Increase speed to medium for another 6 minutes. As you increase the speed, gradually add the remaining water, letting the dough absorb the water. The result should be a smooth and slightly fluid dough.
If you do not have a stand mixer, knead by hand for a few minutes, then add the water and knead again until dough is a smooth and uniform ball. Remove dough, brush with tsp. of olive oil, and place in large bowl.
Cover the bowl with plastic wrap and leave in a warm place for 60–90 minutes, until the dough has doubled in size. (Can also be refrigerated overnight.)
Line a tray with baking paper. Sprinkle flour on a clean surface and divide the dough into 8 equal portions. Roll each portion into a ball of dough and let rest for 10 minutes.
Make each ball of dough into a 12-in.-long (30-cm-long) cylindrical roll. Join the edges of each roll together to create a ring. Press the ends together and place the bagel rings on the prepared baking tray. Gently stretch each ring to create an elliptical shape.

Glaze
Mix baking soda with the lukewarm water to make a glaze, brush over the bagels, and sprinkle sesame seeds on top.
Let bagels rest in a warm place for 1 hour, or until they have doubled in size. Preheat oven to 430°F (220°C).
Bake for 20–25 minutes, until golden-brown. Allow to cool before serving.

SOURDOUGH BAGELS

Jewish immigrants brought the bagel from Eastern Europe to the New World. There, it quickly became a staple of the Jewish community and an inseparable part of U.S. and New York cuisine. That is not quite the way things turned out in Israel, where the bagel never truly entered the canon— but a few Jerusalem bakeries still produce bagels according to Ashkenazi tradition.

INGREDIENTS

3½ oz. (100 g) sourdough starter
  (page 294)
1½ cups (350 ml) cold water
1 tbsp. sugar
1 lb. (500 g) white flour
1 heaping tsp. fine salt
1 tsp. extra virgin olive oil

Topping
½ cup (120 ml) baking soda
½ cup (120 ml) lukewarm water
1 pinch of coarse sea salt

DIRECTIONS

Combine the starter, 1 cup (250 ml) cold water, sugar, flour, and salt in the bowl of a stand mixer. Using the dough hook, knead for 3 minutes at low speed. Increase the speed to medium for another 6 minutes. As you increase the speed, gradually add the remaining water, letting the dough absorb the water. The result should be a smooth and slightly fluid dough. If you do not have a stand mixer, knead by hand for a few minutes, then add water and knead again, until dough becomes a smooth, uniform ball. Remove the dough, brush with the tsp. of olive oil, and transfer to a large bowl.
Cover the bowl with plastic wrap and leave in a warm place for 60–90 minutes, until the dough has doubled in size. (Can also be refrigerated overnight.)
Line a tray with baking paper. Sprinkle flour on a clean surface and divide the dough into 8 equal portions. Roll each portion into a ball of dough and let rest for 10 minutes.
Make each ball of dough into a 12-in.-long (30-cm-long) cylindrical roll. Join the edges of each roll together to create a ring. Press the ends together and place the bagel rings on the prepared baking tray.
In a small bowl, mix the baking soda with ½ cup (120 ml) lukewarm water to make a glaze, brush over the bagels, and sprinkle salt on top.
Let bagels rest in a warm place for 1 hour, or until they have doubled in size. Preheat oven to 430°F (220°C).
Bake the bagels for 20–25 minutes, until golden-brown.
Allow to cool before serving.

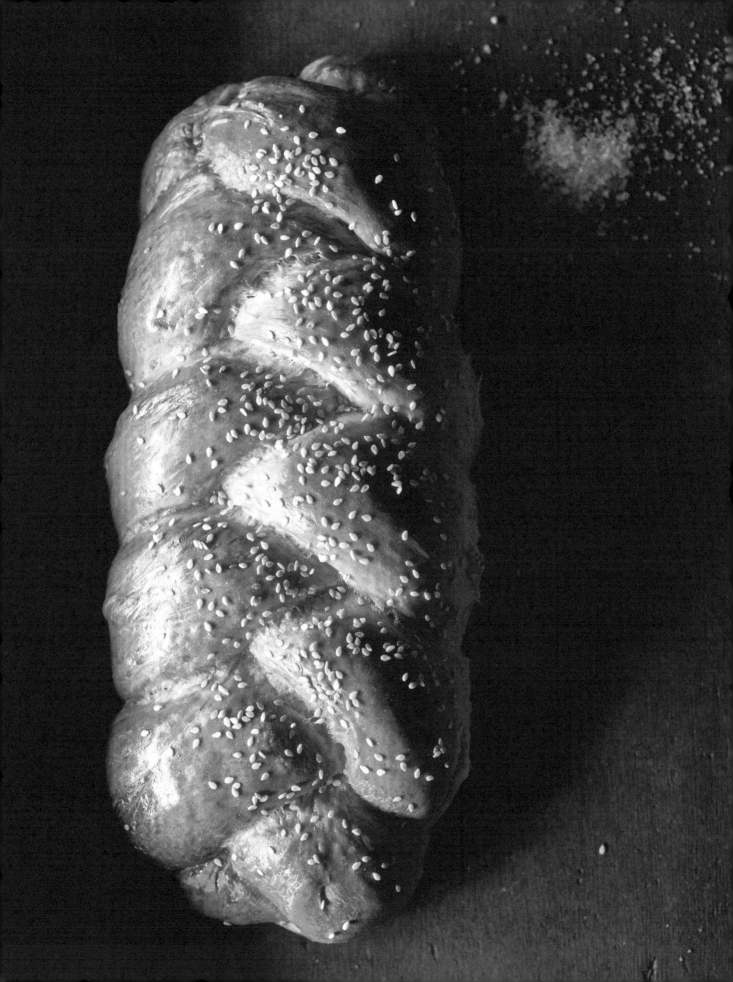

CHALLAH BREAD

One of Judaism's seminal recipes, challah is baked and eaten all over the world by Jews of every age and creed. These days, you might even see a loaf of challah in a non-Jewish bakery window, or challah French toast served up at a hip city café. This recipe yields a sweet challah; for a savory version, use only a single tablespoon of sugar instead of 1¾ oz. (50 grams).

INGREDIENTS

1 lb. (500 g) white flour
¾ oz. (25 g) fresh yeast
1¾ oz. (50 g) sugar
1 heaping tsp. fine salt
9 fl. oz. (260 ml) water
2 tbsp. extra virgin olive oil
1 egg, beaten

DIRECTIONS

Place all ingredients except for the egg in the bowl of a stand mixer. Using the dough hook, knead for 3 minutes at low speed. Increase the speed to medium for another 6 minutes, until the dough is smooth and slightly firm. If you do not have a stand mixer, knead by hand until dough becomes a smooth and uniform ball.

Place the dough in a large, oiled bowl, cover with plastic wrap, and leave to proof in a warm place for 1 to 1½ hours. Once the dough rises, divide into four equal portions.

Roll each portion into a ball on a floured work surface. Roll each ball into a strip 12 in. (30 cm) long, thicker in the center and thinner at the edges. On a sheet of baking paper, place four strips in a row and gather them together at the top, furthest from you. Take the left-most strip and pass it to the right, under the next two strips, then back left over the strip to its left. Take the right-most strip and pass it to the left, under the next two strips (which are already braided), and then back right over the strip to its right. Repeat until you reach the bottom and have formed a neat braid.

Press on the challah end with the side of your palm and remove the uneven edges with your little finger. Make sure to squeeze both ends together and tuck them under the loaf.

Use the baking paper to lift the challah onto a baking tray. Leave the tray in a warm place for 90 minutes, covered with a clean dishtowel, until the dough has tripled in size.

Preheat oven to 340°F (170°C).

Brush evenly with beaten egg. Bake for 40 min. until deep, golden brown. Remove and let cool 15–20 minutes before serving.

SEPHARDIC STUFFED PASTRIES

An ode to the eggplant by an anonymous Jewish poet in eighteenth-century Istanbul has 37 verses describing 36 eggplant dishes. Sephardic Jews and Palestinian Arabs used to say that a woman's worth lay in her ability to cook eggplant 100 different ways. This stuffed pastry common in Sephardic kitchens is just one of them, but it may be the only one you will ever need.

INGREDIENTS

Dough
10½ oz. (300 g) plain flour
7 oz. (200 g) unsalted butter
1 egg
½ tsp. salt

Filling
1 large eggplant, washed
  and dried
1 small onion, finely chopped
1 tsp. salt
¼ cup (60 g) finely chopped
  fresh parsley
½ tsp. sweet paprika
9 oz. (250 g) minced lamb
1 egg, beaten, for baking

DIRECTIONS

Pulse dough ingredients in food processor until a smooth dough ball forms. Remove the dough, wrap with plastic wrap, and refrigerate for 1 hour. Meanwhile, to roast the eggplant, line the stovetop with aluminum foil, and place the eggplant directly on the open flame. Once the skin is charred on one side, use kitchen tongs to turn it over. When the eggplant skin is fully charred, the flesh inside is soft, and it can be pierced with a knife, remove from the heat and place in a colander over a bowl to let cool and drain.
If you do not have a gas stove, slice the eggplant in half, put both halves face down on a baking sheet, and set your oven to broil. Remove eggplant when flesh is soft and skin is charred.
Once eggplant has cooled, cut lengthwise and separate the flesh from the skin using a fork. Do not wash—this will remove the smoky flavor— even if some small pieces of skin remain.
With a heavy knife, chop and mash eggplant into a puree. Place in a bowl.
Add the onion, salt, parsley, and paprika, and mix well.
Add the minced lamb. Mix by hand for a few minutes, then cover and refrigerate for 40 minutes.
Preheat oven to 355°F (180°C) and line a tray with baking paper.
Roll out the dough thinly (1/10 in. or 3 mm) on floured work surface.
With a biscuit cutter, cut out discs 4 in. (10 cm) in diameter.
Place a tbsp. of filling in the middle of each disc.
Fold the edges of the circle upwards and pinch together around the filling to create a flower shape.
Place pastries on tray, brush with beaten egg, bake for 20 minutes until golden brown, and serve.

JERUSALEM KUGEL

Kugel, a slow-cooked noodle or potato pudding, is a typical Ashkenazi Sabbath dish found across Eastern Europe. In Hassidic communities today, the kugel has earned a cult status unusual for Judaism, similar to Christian sacramental bread. A rabbi is believed to imbue the kugel with his spiritual powers, and his followers eat it straight from his hands.

INGREDIENTS

1 lb. (500 g) wide egg-noodles (fettuccine)
¼ cup (60 ml) sunflower oil
1 onion, chopped
¾ cup (170 g) sugar
4 eggs
1 tsp. salt
2 tsp. freshly ground black pepper

DIRECTIONS

Preheat oven to 210°F (100°C).
Bring a pot of saltwater to a boil and cook the noodles according to package instructions.
While the noodles are cooking, heat half the oil in a large saucepan.
Add onion and fry until completely golden.
Add sugar and the remaining oil to the onion, mix well, and cook for 5 minutes over low heat.
Combine the cooked and drained noodles with the onion mixture in a large bowl and let cool.
Beat the eggs, add to the bowl with the salt and pepper, and mix well.
Pour mixture into a loaf tin and cover with aluminum foil.
Bake for 12 hours.
Remove from the oven and allow to cool slightly.
Applying light pressure to the sides of the tin, turn out the kugel onto a dish and serve.

JERUSALEM-STYLE CHICKEN SOFRITO

Every Mediterranean country has its sofrito. Among Jerusalem's Sephardim, sofrito is a soft, juicy roast, usually chicken, served with golden potatoes to absorb the flavors. Sofrito is made by frying each ingredient separately then simmering them together. The chicken produces enough juices to make a stock in which the entire dish cooks, creating an ideal union of flavors.

INGREDIENTS

⅓ cup (80 ml) sunflower oil
1 whole chicken, quartered
8 large potatoes,
   peeled and quartered
1 tsp. ground turmeric
½ tsp. coriander seeds
½ tsp. baharat spice mix
   (page 19)
1 tsp. salt
½ tsp. freshly ground
   white pepper
2 tbsp. water

DIRECTIONS

Preheat oven to 320°F (160°C).
Heat a heavy, oven-safe casserole dish or cast-iron pot on the stove and add the oil.
Fry chicken quarters on all sides, until slightly golden.
Remove chicken and set aside.
Fry the potatoes on all sides, until slightly golden. Remove potatoes and set aside.
Discard the oil in the casserole dish. Place half the potatoes in the dish, making an even layer. Put chicken pieces in next, then the rest of the potatoes.
Mix turmeric, coriander, baharat, salt, and pepper with the water, then pour it over the chicken and potatoes in the dish.
Cover and bake for 2½ hours. Serve hot out of the oven.

LAMB AND FENNEL PATTIES

Fennel's aniseed taste is a familiar characteristic of many Mediterranean dishes. The root vegetable can be delicate or sharp, depending on how it is prepared, and roasting brings out its deeply sweet, earthy notes. Paired with lamb in this dish, fennel becomes a crucial aromatic flavor component while also providing contrasting color to the burnished meat.

INGREDIENTS

For the patties
2 fennel bulbs
1 lb. (500 g) minced lamb
2 garlic cloves, minced
4 tbsp. finely chopped
   fresh parsley
½ tsp. grated lemon zest
1 tsp. salt
½ tsp. freshly ground
   black pepper

For the roasted fennel
4 fennel bulbs, sliced lengthwise
   into six wedges
2 cups (500 ml) chicken stock
   (page 289)
3 tbsp. extra virgin olive oil
½ tsp. coarse salt
½ tsp. freshly ground
   black pepper

DIRECTIONS

Remove the stalks from the two fennel bulbs and chop the bulbs finely, preferably in a food processor.
Put the chopped fennel in a bowl, add the rest of the patty ingredients, and mix well until texture is somewhat sticky. Refrigerate for 1 hour.
Preheat oven to 390°F (200°C).
Roll the mixture into 12 patties. Arrange in a roasting pan, placing the fennel wedges between them.
Pour chicken stock over the patties and fennel, drizzle them with olive oil, and sprinkle with salt and pepper.
Roast for approx. 35 minutes, or until the fennel wedges are soft, then serve.

LAMB SHAWARMA WITH TAHINI

Shawarma, a popular Turkish street snack, has been happily adopted into Israel's regional cuisine. The original recipe uses lamb meat, but in Israel you can also find it with chicken or turkey meat seasoned with lamb fat; the spices can also vary from those used in Turkey, but that is the beauty of shawarma: in a pita or on a plate, each region and each chef makes it unique.

INGREDIENTS

1¾ lb. (800 g) leg of lamb, bone-in

1 red onion, thinly sliced

4 garlic cloves, minced

1 tsp. finely chopped fresh green Anaheim chili, deseeded

1 tsp. coarse sea salt

1 tsp. freshly ground black pepper

½ tsp. ground cumin

3 large ripe tomatoes

2 tbsp. freshly squeezed lemon juice

¼ cup (60 ml) prepared tahini sauce (page 290)

2 tbsp. extra virgin olive oil

3 tbsp. finely chopped fresh parsley

DIRECTIONS

Cut the lamb into thin slices, resembling escalopes.

Heat a large frying pan over high heat.

Dry-roast lamb slices for two minutes on each side. Transfer to a plate.

Add onion, garlic, chili, salt, pepper, and cumin to the frying pan and dry-roast for 3–5 minutes, stirring constantly, until onion is golden.

Place lamb slices on a cutting board and cut into ⅕-in.-wide (½-cm-wide) strips with a heavy knife.

Reheat the pan until the spice mix bubbles. Add the lamb slices and fry, stirring constantly, until the slices brown and are slightly crisp.

Cut the tomatoes in half and squeeze their juices into the pan as if you were squeezing a lemon.

Add lemon juice and cook for 3–5 minutes, until the sauce thickens.

Remove pan from the heat. Pour the prepared tahini over the lamb, drizzle with olive oil, sprinkle parsley on top, and serve.

ACORN SQUASH STUFFED WITH RICE AND LAMB

Beloved across the Middle East, stuffed squash is one of those satisfying dishes that look a lot more complex than they are. This is a modern variation on a traditional recipe from the kitchens of Jewish communities in central Asia (hence the basmati rice). Acorn squash are ideal for this recipe, as they have a bright flavor and hold their shape well after cooking.

INGREDIENTS

Stuffing
½ lb. (500 g) minced lamb
½ lb. (500 g) basmati rice, cooked
2 carrots, coarsely grated
½ cup (100 g) canned chickpeas
1 onion, finely chopped
½ cup (15 g) finely chopped
   fresh parsley
1 tbsp. chopped garlic
¼ cup (60 ml) pomegranate
   concentrate
1 tsp. ground cinnamon
2 tsp. salt
1 tsp. freshly ground
   black pepper

3 medium acorn squash,
   halved and deseeded

DIRECTIONS

Preheat oven to 320°F (160°C).
Combine stuffing ingredients in a large bowl and mix well.
Place squash halves in two roasting trays, face up, and fill with
the stuffing mixture.
Cover with a double layer of aluminum foil and bake for 4 hours.
Remove aluminum foil, increase oven temperature to 390°F (200°C),
and roast for another 10 minutes.
Remove from oven and arrange on a large dish to serve.

ONIONS STUFFED WITH MEAT AND RICE

In Western cuisine, onions are rarely used as more than a garnish or a sauce ingredient, and that is a shame. The cooking process tones down their overwhelming sharpness, and they make a wonderful shell for all kinds of tasty fillings. The crushed tomatoes that surround the onions add another layer of flavor and ensure that nothing dries out during the roasting process.

INGREDIENTS

For the stuffing
1⅓ lb. (600 g) ground beef
2 garlic cloves, minced
2 tbsp. thyme
¼ cup (60 ml) chopped
    fresh parsley
1 tsp. salt
½ tsp. freshly ground
    black pepper

3 large onions

For roasting
2 tbsp. olive oil
1 lb. (500 g) canned, crushed
    tomatoes

DIRECTIONS

Fill a medium saucepan three-quarters full of water and bring to a boil.
Prepare ice water in a bowl.
Combine all the stuffing ingredients and mix well.
Peel the onions and cut each lengthwise, almost but not completely to the center, so that they hold together while boiling.
Place onions in the boiling water and cook for 3–4 minutes.
When onions are soft, remove with a slotted spoon and place them in the ice water.
Let the onions cool for five minutes, then remove from the water and carefully peel off the layers, one by one.
Brush a rectangular roasting tray with olive oil and preheat oven to 390°F (200°C).
Fill each layer of onion with a heaping spoonful of stuffing.
Press each layer into an elliptical shape and place on the roasting tray, filling the spaces in between with crushed tomatoes.
Roast for 35–40 minutes, until onions are soft and golden-brown, and serve hot.

LAMB CASSEROLE WITH LEMON, ROSEMARY, AND GARLIC

This dish is the essence of typical regional flavors. Lemon, garlic, and rosemary brighten up the lamb's earthy flavor, while olive oil and white wine bring everything together, mixing with the juices to make a truly decadent sauce that pairs well with couscous, rice, or potatoes, and is just as tasty sopped up with bread at the end of the meal.

INGREDIENTS

- ¼ cup (60 ml) extra virgin olive oil
- 2 lb. (1 kg) bone-in leg of lamb, chopped into 1½-in. (4-cm) chunks
- 4 tbsp. garlic cloves, minced
- 1 lemon, washed and unpeeled, cut into ⅓-in. (1-cm) cubes
- 1 heaping tsp. coarse sea salt
- 1 tsp. freshly ground black pepper
- ½ bottle dry white wine
- 3 sprigs rosemary

DIRECTIONS

Preheat oven to 320°F (160°C).

Heat half the olive oil over high heat in a heavy oven-safe casserole dish or cast-iron pot.

Add the lamb chunks a few at a time, and sauté until lightly browned on all sides, then remove and place on a plate. (Sauté only a few chunks at a time to avoid lowering the temperature of the oil.)

When all chunks are browned, return to the casserole dish with all the juices.

Add garlic, lemon cubes, salt, and pepper, and cook over high heat for three minutes.

Add white wine and the remainder of the olive oil and bring to a boil.

Let boil for 3 minutes until alcohol has evaporated.

Remove from the heat, add the rosemary sprigs, cover with a lid, and place in the oven.

Bake for 3 hours, until lamb is very soft, and serve hot.

MACARONI HAMIN

For centuries, Jewish communities adopted culinary customs from the societies around them, often modifying them to fit kosher law (see page 167). Hamin, a type of all-in-one-pot, whatever's-left-over stew, is one of the few dishes found in all Jewish communities. Beloved by all, it has somehow become particularly associated with Jerusalem.

INGREDIENTS

1 tbsp. tomato puree
1 tsp. sweet paprika
3 tbsp. extra virgin olive oil
2 tsp. fine salt
2 tsp. freshly ground
    black pepper
12 chicken drumsticks
6 medium potatoes
1 lb. (500 g) dry macaroni
4 eggs, beaten

DIRECTIONS

In a large bowl, combine tomato puree, paprika, olive oil, salt, and pepper.
Add the chicken pieces and mix well until evenly coated.
Cover the bowl and let marinate in the refrigerator for 1 hour.
Peel the potatoes and cut crosswise into ⅕-in.-thick (½-cm-thick) slices.
Place in a bowl, and cover with water to prevent darkening.
Boil water with 1 tbsp. of salt in a large saucepan, cook the macaroni until just al dente, then drain.
Preheat oven to 250°F (120°C).
Oil a heavy, oven-safe casserole dish or cast-iron pot and arrange potato slices on the bottom. Cover slices with half of the cooked macaroni.
Top macaroni evenly with the chicken pieces, saving the marinade, then cover the chicken with the rest of the macaroni.
Add beaten eggs to the bowl of marinade, mix well, then pour into the casserole dish.
Cut a circle of greaseproof paper the diameter of the casserole and cover the top layer of macaroni to keep the dish from drying out in the oven.
Cover with a tight-fitting lid and bake for 12 hours (ideally overnight).
Serve directly from the casserole or turn out onto a large serving platter.

GOOD TO KNOW

What you see in the picture may not be what you have come to think of as "macaroni," but many Israelis—especially older generations—use the word to refer to any type of pasta.

ROSEWATER MALABI CUSTARD WITH WILD BERRY SYRUP

A classic dessert inspired by Arabic cuisine of the Middle Ages, this pudding has a bright, gorgeous look and a bold, un-expected flavor. It eschews gelatin (which in most cases is not kosher if made from pigs) in favor of cornstarch, which stiffens the heavy cream just enough to form a custard but still leaves its texture smooth and silken.

INGREDIENTS

Custard
8¾ oz. (250 g) heavy whipping cream
8½ fl. oz. (250 ml) milk
3 tbsp. sugar
3 tbsp. cornstarch, dissolved in 2 tbsp. cold milk
4 drops rosewater extract

Sauce
8¾ oz. (250 g) mixed wild berries
2 tbsp. sugar
¼ cup (60 ml) water
2 tbsp. crème de cassis

DIRECTIONS

Bring the cream, milk, and sugar to a boil in a small saucepan.
Add the dissolved cornstarch and cook over low heat, whisking constantly, until mixture is smooth, thick, and bubbly.
Remove from heat, add the rosewater extract, stir well, and portion the mix into 8 bowls.
Cool to room temperature, then cover the bowls and refrigerate for at least 2 hours.
Bring sauce ingredients to a boil in a small saucepan.
Reduce the heat and simmer for 10 minutes.
Remove from heat and let cool to room temperature.
When the 2 hours are up, remove each bowl from the refrigerator and swirl a ⅓-in.-thick (1-cm-thick) layer of berry sauce over each pudding before serving.

ALMOND POUND CAKE

Simple and satisfying, pound cake is a go-to dessert or teatime snack in many cultures. Almonds are the most popular nut in Israel, appearing in hundreds of recipes from both Arab and Jewish-Sephardic cuisines. Here, they are used to give the world-beloved pound cake a regional twist, adding flavor without changing the cake's dense, bouncy texture.

INGREDIENTS

5 oz. (140 g) white flour

3½ oz. (100 g) blanched almonds, ground

1 tsp. baking powder

1 tsp. baking soda

7 oz. (200 g) unsalted butter at room temperature

4¼ oz. (120 g) sugar

6 drops almond extract

3 eggs

1 tbsp. freshly squeezed lemon juice

DIRECTIONS

Preheat oven to 340°F (170°C).

Line a 10-in.-long (25-cm-long) loaf tin with baking paper.

Sift flour, almonds, baking powder, and baking soda into a large bowl.

Beat butter and sugar in a standing mixer or in a deep bowl with a hand-held mixer, at medium speed, until light and fluffy. While beating, alternate between adding 2 drops of the almond extract and 1 egg until both are fully incorporated and the batter is smooth.

Gradually add the sifted dry ingredients and beat in.

Add lemon juice and beat until smooth.

Pour the mix into the prepared loaf tin and bake for 40 minutes, until a toothpick inserted in the center comes out clean.

Remove from the oven, cover with a clean dishtowel, and let cool for 40 minutes.

MARZIPAN COOKIES

Israel's most popular nut, almonds find their way into just about everything. These cookies are not really marzipan in texture (they have little to do with the dry, crumbly, and often artificially-colored masses children are presented with on holidays in parts of the world), but they do replace white flour with ground almonds (almond flour) for a lovely, subtle effect.

INGREDIENTS

8 ¾ oz. (250 g) sugar
3 egg whites, at room temperature
10½ oz. (300 g) blanched almonds, ground into almond flour
½ tsp. baking powder
5 drops almond extract
½ cup (60 g) powdered sugar

DIRECTIONS

In a bowl, mix sugar, egg whites, ground almonds, baking powder, and almond extract until mixture is slightly sticky.
Refrigerate for 30 minutes.
Meanwhile, preheat oven to 355°F (180 °C) and line a tray with baking paper.
Place the powdered sugar in a small bowl.
Remove the mixture from the refrigerator. With moist hands, roll the mixture into balls about the size of a ping-pong ball. Then roll each ball in the powdered sugar and place on the baking tray, spacing them at least ⅘ in. (2 cm) apart.
Bake for 13 minutes, then remove and allow to cool.
Once cool, the cookies will have the right texture, and can be eaten right away or stored in an airtight container for up to 3 days.

ORANGE SEMOLINA CAKE

Basbousa, a dense semolina cake soaked in sugar syrup, is a common dessert in Arabic cuisine, sold in many confectionary stores and from street food carts specializing in sweets. Here it is given a modern update with the addition of oranges (in the form of juice and blossom extract) as well as an attractive dusting of coconut for an additional flavor contrast.

INGREDIENTS

Cake
5 eggs
2¾ oz. (80 g) sugar
5⅓ oz. (150 g) unsalted butter, melted
3½ oz. (100 g) plain flour
5⅓ oz. (150 g) semolina
2½ oz. (70 g) desiccated coconut, plus ⅓ cup (80 ml) for decoration
1 tsp. baking powder
7 fl. oz. (200 ml) orange juice
6 drops orange blossom extract

Syrup
¾ cup (180 ml) water
5 oz. (150 g) sugar
2 tbsp. freshly squeezed lemon juice

DIRECTIONS

Preheat oven to 340°F (170°C).
Line a 12-in.-long (30-cm-long) loaf tin with baking paper.
Place eggs and sugar in the bowl of a standing mixer. Using the whisk attachment, beat for 6–7 minutes until mixture is fluffy.
(Alternatively, place in a deep bowl and beat using a hand mixer.)
Add the butter gradually and beat until fully absorbed.
Sift flour, semolina, coconut, and baking powder and orange blossom extract into a bowl.
Alternate between adding the sifted ingredients and the orange juice, beating between each addition until batter is smooth and uniform.
Pour batter into the prepared loaf tin and bake in the oven for 40 minutes.
30 minutes into the baking time, combine syrup ingredients in a small saucepan and bring to a boil, then remove from heat.
Remove cake from the oven and pour syrup over it.
Scatter desiccated coconut on top and let cool for 40 minutes before serving.
Can be kept for up to 48 hours in an airtight container.

CITRUS POPPY SEED STRUDEL

This update of the Central and Eastern European dessert most commonly known as strudel—a rich, melt-in-your-mouth pastry consisting almost entirely of filling surrounded by a thin layer of dough—uses oranges three ways for a zesty contrast to the earthy poppy seeds. A favorite among Ashkenazi Jews, poppy seeds have become a symbol of the Purim holiday.

INGREDIENTS

Filling
7 oz. (200 g) ground poppy seeds
⅔ cup (150 ml) milk
3½ oz. (100 g) unsalted butter
3½ oz. (100 g) castor or
  superfine sugar
2 tbsp. orange liqueur
6 drops orange blossom extract
½ tsp. orange zest
2 eggs, beaten

Dough
10½ oz. (300 g) plain flour
3½ oz. (200 g) unsalted butter
1 egg
⅓ cup (40 g) powdered sugar
½ tsp. vanilla extract
1 pinch of salt

DIRECTIONS

Place the ground poppy seeds, milk, butter, and sugar in a small saucepan and bring to a boil. Reduce heat and cook, stirring constantly, for 3 minutes. Remove saucepan from the heat. Add orange ingredients. Mix well and set aside to cool for 15 minutes.
Add beaten eggs and stir well to combine. Refrigerate for 30 minutes.
Cover your work surface with plastic wrap. Place the filling on one side in an even line 10 in. (25 cm) long. Carefully roll the plastic wrap to enfold the filling, creating an elongated sausage-like shape.
Place it on a flat surface in the freezer for about 4 hours, until frozen.
Meanwhile, place dough ingredients in a food processor. Pulse until a smooth ball of dough forms.
Wrap the dough ball in plastic wrap and refrigerate.
Once the filling is frozen, preheat oven to 320°F (160°C).
On a floured work surface, roll dough out very thin with rolling pin.
Trim the sides to create a dough square measuring 10 × 10 in. (25 × 25 cm).
Remove filling from freezer, peel off plastic wrap, and place along edge of dough. Roll dough around filling until completely wrapped.
Line a 10-in. (25-cm) loaf tin with baking paper. Place the roll in the tin.
Brush beaten egg on top of the roll. Bake for 40 minutes, until golden.
Let cool for 40 minutes before to serving. Will keep up to 48 hours in an airtight container.

THE SOUTH

LEBANON
Acre
Safed
Haifa
Nazareth Tiberias
Sea of Galilee
SYRIA

Mediterranean Sea

Jerusalem
Dead Sea

Gaza
ISRAEL

The Negev
JORDAN

EGYPT
Arava

Red Sea

DESERT TRADITIONS AND HIGH-TECH FARMING

Sandwiched between Egypt and Jordan and buttressed by the Red Sea, the South is a culturally diverse area, where culinary traditions hark back to North African Jews as well as the cultures that have settled the Mediterranean over millennia. Nomad recipes rely on animals and tools that could be taken along for the journey, while the most lasting, staid structures might just be the vineyards and greenhouses where grapes and olives, peppers and tomatoes, and even strawberries grow.

Southern Israel's vast desert expanse hides many secrets, but the most surprising may be just how lush and fruitful it is. Hidden among the dunes, dotted with nomads' tents and some of the country's earliest settlements, are greenhouses bursting with life, which take advantage of age-old irrigation techniques repurposed for the modern era.

Northern Israel is the country at its most lush, while Tel Aviv is a shining beacon of a metropolis, its streets flush with promise and its people rich with ideas and ambition. Jerusalem's sandy buildings, stone alleyways, hidden gardens, and bustling souks whisper of thousands of years of history and fervent devotion. But when you picture Israel, it is often the deserts of the South that come to mind, silent and resilient, dotted with nomads' tents, the remains of ancient cities, and some of Israel's earliest settlements, Bedouin secrets hidden among the dunes.

Some of these secrets, of course, are surprisingly delicious for such a seemingly barren area—the Negev and Arava deserts, where very little rain falls. Nomadic tribes like the Bedouin whose traditional livelihood was herding camels and sheep, based their cuisines on the animals and tools they could bring with them, very often seeming to conjure dishes directly out of the fire. Though many of them have exchanged their tents for permanent housing in recent years, these dishes stayed with them, perhaps updated for a contemporary audience by their children, or preserved for special occasions as they once

In the South, the harvest owes much more to mankind and human ingenuity than to nature.

Previous page, right: **The narrow, winding Scorpion's Pass in the eastern Negev desert is a recognized heritage site in Israel and, until the mid-20th century, was on the primary route that connected the Red Sea port town of Eilat to central Israel.** This page: **Children learn the value of agriculture early at organic greenhouses like this one, run by Ronit Elazari, a preschool agriculture teacher.**
Opposite page: **Year-round lush plantlife contributes to a wide variety of dishes.**

The Ein Yahav settlement in the northern Arava is home to many greenhouses like this one, growing tomatoes with a wide spectrum of flavors and colors.

Fruits and vegetables flourish in the Arava's fields and greenhouses, benefitting from the region's nearly endless summer.

were generations ago. To this day, in Bedouin villages, elderly women still cook the traditional cuisine of the nomad. Flat, thin pita bread is baked on the saj, a convex tin pan placed over a campfire. Afig, a pungent cheese of dried goat or sheep's milk is made in the springtime and left to dry in the sun and the hot desert air—the dried cheese chunks, never refrigerated, are eaten year-round, with a little water added to restore their moistness. Then there is bsisa, an ancient Bedouin "energy snack" with its sharp, smoky aroma, made of toasted ground flour mixed with olive oil, water, sugar, and salt. In the past, even when roaming tribes could not stop to light a fire, they knew they could rely on nutritious bsisa for a quick hunger fix.

Traditionally, the Bedouin ate meat sparingly, instead relying on their flocks to provide the milk and wool necessary for living. Meat was reserved for holidays, special occasions, or to welcome an honored guest, but when it was

INTRODUCING...
SHAKSHUKA

If tomatoes could choose their bedfellows, Israelis like to imagine they would lie down with eggs. That is because this prodigious pairing yields a dish that has become a favorite not just in Israel, but all across the Middle East. The debate rages on about who came up with shakshuka (recipe page 256) first—the Turks, Tunisians, Moroccans, Yemenis, and Libyans all claim it as their own. But one thing is certain: everyone has a preferred version these days. This simple dish, whose name means "all mixed up" in Hebrew, can be found all over Israel, from cozy home kitchens to chic cafés. It is a one-pan dish (ideally it should be served sizzling in the pan it was cooked in) that goes with just about everything, and it is a great way to use up all those overly ripe tomatoes lying around your kitchen.

When you picture Israel, it is often the deserts that come to mind, silent and resilient, dotted with no-mads' tents, the remains of ancient cities, and some of Israel's earliest settlements.

Shivta National Park houses the remains of a Byzantine city—a flourishing center of wine production in ancient times.

Like their Nabatean forefathers, the Negev's few thousand modern farmers have overcome the arid desert climate with sophisticated modern agriculture.

GOT A STRAWBERRY CRAVING?

A hardy crop with a reliable annual yield, strawberries have long been one of Israel's most successful exports. Now they have competition, though, as growers in Egypt, Morocco, and even the Gaza Strip ready their produce for an increasingly strawberry-hungry world market. Israel keeps ahead of the curve by introducing new technologies that will extend the strawberry growing season, possibly even making it a year-round affair, and allow strawberries to thrive in any number of unusual, high-tech setups (like the hanging strawberry greenhouses shown above).

offered, it was cooked directly in the ground, according to an ancient method called matfuna, Arabic for "buried." In a process reminiscent of barbecue in the southern United States, the Bedouin take advantage of the low but steady heat of a dying fire by digging a pit, lining it with glowing embers, and placing whole lambs, young goats, or chickens on top. Covering it all with embers and sand, they leave it to go about their daily business. Some hours later, when they return to uncover their treasure, the meat is soft, succulent, and falling-off-the-bone, with a distinctly smoky flavor.

Farming and trading also formed the backbone of the economy in this area over centuries. In fact, two millennia ago, tens of thousands of farmers lived in the Negev and tended vineyards and orchards, despite the arid climate. The Nabateans were renowned for the camel trains that traversed the Incense Route from southern Arabia through Petra to the Gaza harbor, carrying frank-incense and myrrh, peaches and ginger, pepper, Indian silk, and exotic spices from Africa.

After the Roman conquest, the fortresses and trading stations along the Incense Route became permanent cities. The Nabateans, skilled in irrigation, grew flourishing crops in an area with just a few inches of annual rainfall. Their technique involved collecting winter rain and floodwater runoff and

The Nabateans, skilled in irrigation,
grew flourishing crops in an area
with just a few inches of annual rainfall.

channeling it into a complex system of terraces, small dams, and canals, and on to small plots where the region's famous produce grew. In this way, they managed to create lush oases within the desert, where wheat, barley, figs, and fruit trees thrived, joined by grapes and olives for wine and olive oil. In turn, this artificial abundance infuses the dishes they brought to their tables with color and flavor, celebrating a harvest that owes much more to mankind and human ingenuity than pure nature.

Like their Nabatean forefathers, the Negev's few thousand modern farmers have overcome the arid desert climate. Their sophisticated modern agriculture also allows vineyards to thrive, growing grapes alongside olive groves, as nearby flocks of sheep produce the milk that goes into salty, pungent, crumbly and hard cheeses. Fruits and vegetables flourish in the Arava's fields and greenhouses, benefitting from the region's nearly endless summer.

Locally grown eggplants, melons, and dates are renowned worldwide, though arguably the region's best known crops are its dozens of peppers and tomatoes, both heirloom and modern varieties. Hardly known 300 years ago, today they are inseparable components of new Israeli cuisine as well as just about every regional cuisine in the Mediterranean. Arava tomatoes and peppers are shipped

Above: **Scenes from a desert farm near the ancient city of Shivta include a surprising amount of colorful vegetation.** Top right: **A view to the desert.** Bottom right: **A Bedouin woman prepares meals at the farm.**

A simple, traditional spread of flatbread, hummus with pine nuts, and falafel makes a tasty and nourishing midday meal.

The South is thriving, proving that different cultures can exist side by side, and that even a little bit of water does wonders for the driest landscapes.

The Negev and Arava deserts hold surprisingly delicious secrets for such a seemingly barren area.

Left: **Farmer and cheesemaker Daniel Kornmehl proudly shows off the finished product—a round of hard, pungent goats' milk cheese encased in rind.**

to the narrow coastal strip of southern Israel and to Ashdod and Ashkelon, two coastal cities with a large population of North African Jews who came to Israel in the 1950s and 1960s.

In the homes and restaurants of these two cities, traditional delights like shakshuka (see page 255), spicy fish with tomato and pepper sauce, Tunisian sandwiches (see page 252), and festive couscous dishes (see page 268), are prepared and eaten with great reverence for their past as well as evident enjoyment of their rich flavors. The deserts, cities, and nomad communities of the South are thriving, proving once and for all that different cultures can exist side by side, and that even a little bit of water does wonders for the driest landscapes.

Grazing, free-roaming goats provide milk—a precious raw ingredient in cheesemaking.

FLAVORS OF THE DESERT

Recipes from the South incorporate fresh fruits and vegetables straight from the greenhouse, grilled, cured, roasted, and marinated for maximum flavor, or simply sliced thinly to allow their raw charm to shine through. Meat, poultry, and fish all make an appearance, alongside a couple of age-old classics like the favorite breakfast dish shakshuka and the ubiquitous falafel and kebab skewers.

The ingredients for this herb omelet (page 178) came from Ronit Elazari's greenhouse in the Arava desert.

ASSORTED TOMATO SALAD

There is nothing quite as pleasing as a sun-ripened tomato, and this salad takes full advantage of the beloved fruit (often wrongly called a vegetable). The salad's ingenious use of tomatoes in two ways—both fresh to celebrate their natural aroma, and roasted to concentrate their sweetness— hits all the right notes. Sheep's milk cheese is a necessary counterpoint.

INGREDIENTS

1 cup (150 g) cherry tomatoes
1 tsp. fine salt
½ tsp. freshly ground
    black pepper
6 large, ripe tomatoes
1 cup (150 g) yellow cherry
    tomatoes
4 tbsp. extra virgin olive oil
2 tbsp. pomegranate
    concentrate
¼ cup (30 g) basil leaves,
    cut into ribbons
2 tbsp. oregano leaves
¼ cup (30 g) sheep's milk
    feta cheese, coarsely grated

DIRECTIONS

Preheat oven to 480°F (250°C).
Line a roasting tray with baking paper. Cut the cherry tomatoes in half and arrange on the tray, cut sides up.
Season tomatoes with half the amount of salt and pepper and roast for 12–14 minutes, until golden brown.
Meanwhile, cut each large tomato into 8 slices and halve the yellow cherry tomatoes. Combine in a large bowl. Add olive oil and pomegranate concentrate and mix well.
Transfer the mix to a large serving bowl and place the roasted tomatoes on top with their roasting juices.
Add basil and oregano leaves, sprinkle on grated feta, and serve.

MELON, GOAT CHEESE, AND MINT SALAD

You might think you are looking at cucumber salad, and you would not be far off. Cucumber and melon are distant cousins; their crunchy flesh shares the same mellow sweetness and green glow. Here, lemon juice and lemon verbena provide a touch of acidity and aroma, goat or sheep's milk cheese contrasts with a smooth pungency, and chili adds a touch of heat.

INGREDIENTS

1 small honeydew melon,
  cut into ⅓-in. (1-cm) cubes
2 tbsp. finely chopped
  fresh mint leaves
½ tsp. grated lemon zest
½ tsp. finely chopped fresh red
  Anaheim chili, deseeded
1 tbsp. freshly squeezed
  lemon juice
½ tsp. finely chopped
  lemon verbena leaves
2 tbsp. extra virgin olive oil,
  plus 1 tbsp. more for drizzling
½ tsp. coarse sea salt
7 oz. (200 g) grated hard goat
  cheese or Greek sheep's milk
  feta cheese

DIRECTIONS

Combine all ingredients except for the cheese in a large serving bowl. Mix gently with your hands, taking care not to crush the melon cubes. Scatter the cheese and drizzle 1 tbsp. of olive oil on top, then serve.

WARM POTATO SALAD WITH GREEN BEANS AND OLIVES

This dish takes a few components of the classic Mediterranean salad niçoise—the best parts, really—and serves them alone, instead of as a topping. The result is a warming, comforting side dish that will somehow feel both familiar and unusual upon first bite. It would pair well with other meze as part of a larger meal, but is also satisfying enough to be the star of the show on its own.

INGREDIENTS

14 oz. (400 g) small potatoes,
   peeled and halved lengthwise
2 tbsp. olive oil
1 tbsp. coarse salt,
   plus ½ tsp. for roasting
½ tsp. freshly ground
   black pepper
14 oz. (400 g) fresh green beans,
   trimmed

Dressing
1 tbsp. Dijon mustard
3 tbsp. olive oil
1 tbsp. pomegranate
   concentrate
1 tbsp. freshly squeezed
   lemon juice
1 tbsp. thyme leaves
4 tbsp. finely chopped
   fresh parsley
½ tsp. fine salt
½ tsp. freshly ground
   black pepper
½ cup (100 g) Kalamata olives,
   pitted

DIRECTIONS

Preheat oven to 428°F (220°C).
Line a roasting tray with baking paper. Arrange potatoes on the tray, cut side up. Drizzle with olive oil and sprinkle ½ teaspoon salt and the ground pepper.
Roast for 25–30 minutes, until potatoes are golden and soft enough to pierce with a fork.
Meanwhile, fill a medium bowl with ice water.
Fill a large saucepan with 2 qt. (2 l) of water. Add one tablespoon of coarse salt and bring to a boil. Add the beans and cook for 7–8 minutes, until al dente.
Remove the beans from the pan with a slotted spoon and shock in the ice water for 5 minutes.
Place all the dressing ingredients except the olives in a jar, close it, and shake well until the dressing is smooth.
Combine the potatoes, green beans, and olives in a large serving bowl. Pour the dressing on top, mix gently, taking care to leave the potatoes intact, and serve.

ARUGULA AND RAW ARTICHOKE SALAD

The artichoke is a popular and beloved ingredient in Jewish North African cuisine, where it is usually served cooked. Diners are often shocked to find it can be served raw, though, and that the thin slicing makes it not only edible but pleasantly crunchy, with a hint of sweetness and a light bitterness that fits in wonderfully with the arugula leaves.

INGREDIENTS

8 fresh artichokes
½ lemon
1 tsp. fine salt
½ tsp. fresh red Anaheim chili,
   sliced into thin rings
Juice of 3 lemons
7 oz. (200 g) arugula leaves,
   washed and dried
3 tbsp. extra virgin olive oil
½ cup (70 g) dry-roasted
   pine nuts

DIRECTIONS

To prep the artichokes
Place each artichoke on a cutting board and, using a serrated knife, cut a thin layer around its circumference. Pull off the leaves, until most have been removed, revealing the artichoke heart. Using the knife, separate the heart from the rest of the leaves and trim the stem slightly, leaving only a small part attached.
Fill a bowl with water and the juice of the lemon half.
Place each artichoke heart in the water as you prep the next.

To make the salad
Cut the artichoke hearts into paper-thin slices (preferably using a mandoline slicer) and place in a bowl with the salt, chili, and lemon juice. Mix together and let the artichoke hearts marinate for 1 hour.
Arrange a layer of artichoke slices in a serving dish and cover with a layer of arugula leaves. Repeat until the dish is fully layered.
In a small bowl, mix half of the remaining marinade with the olive oil, pour over the salad. Scatter with the dry-roasted pine nuts and serve.

MARINATED EGGPLANT

This beloved dish originates in the Balkans, but has become an essential component of Israeli cuisine. A simple, stunning eggplant variation, it makes a great addition to any meze spread (pair it with classics like hummus, falafel, or stuffed grape leaves). Use it as an accompaniment to roasted meat and fish dishes, and you may find it outshines the main course.

INGREDIENTS

3 large eggplants
3 tbsp. olive oil
1 tsp. coarse salt
1 tsp. freshly ground
  black pepper

Marinade
2 tbsp. olive oil
1 tbsp. honey
3 tbsp. red wine vinegar
2 tbsp. chopped fresh parsley
1 tbsp. thyme leaves
3 garlic cloves, sliced
1 tsp. fine salt
½ tsp. finely chopped fresh
  green Anaheim chili, deseeded

DIRECTIONS

Preheat oven to 430°F (220°C).
Line a roasting tray with baking paper.
Cut eggplants into ⅓-in.-thick (1-cm-thick) slices and arrange on the prepared tray.
Pour olive oil over the slices and season with salt and pepper.
Roast for 20–25 minutes, until eggplants are soft and golden brown.
Meanwhile, combine all the marinade ingredients and mix thoroughly.
Place eggplants in a deep dish.
Pour marinade over the eggplants, cover the dish, and let the eggplants marinate for at least 2 hours, ideally 6 hours.
Transfer to a serving dish, garnish with even more parsley as desired, and serve.

CURED OCEAN BONITO

The cooking method for this dish has been popular in the Mediterranean for centuries. Its traditional role is to preserve fresh fish. The cured fish can then be served in small pieces as a starter, or used in salads and sandwiches. Kept in the refrigerator, covered in oil, it will last for a few weeks, and the oil can later be strained and reused.

INGREDIENTS

1 ocean bonito, weighing around 2 lb. (approx. 1 kg), cut along the bone into 1½–2 in. (4 to 5 cm) thick slices, or several smaller fish
2 quarts (approx. 2 liters) extra virgin olive oil
Strip of peel from half a lemon
½ tsp. allspice
1 tbsp. coarse sea salt

DIRECTIONS

Place fish in a low, wide saucepan.
Pour the olive oil over it and add the strip of lemon peel, allspice, and salt.
Place the pan on the lowest heat possible.
Cover and simmer for 50 minutes.
Let cool to room temperature.
Transfer contents to a suitable container. Covered in oil, the fish will keep for several weeks in the refrigerator.

TUNISIAN CURED FISH SALAD

This captivating dish of potatoes, cured fish and preserved lemon is a specialty of Tunisian Jews. The surprising taste combination is a salty, savory ode to the sea. Originally, the ingredients were mixed together and sandwiched between two slices of bread—a street food aptly named a "Tunisian sandwich"—but it feels just right as a salad, too.

INGREDIENTS

4 large potatoes,
    washed and unpeeled
4 ripe red tomatoes
14 oz. (400 g) cured ocean bonito
    (page 250)
2 hard boiled eggs, quartered
1 small red onion, thinly sliced

Dressing
3 tbsp. extra virgin olive oil
2 tbsp. finely chopped
    preserved lemon (page 294)
2 tbsp. freshly squeezed
    lemon juice
1 tsp. fine salt
1 tsp. freshly ground
    black pepper
1 tsp. harissa, to taste
    (page 293)

Parsley leaves for garnishing

DIRECTIONS

Preheat oven to 390°F (200°C).
Wrap the potatoes in aluminum foil and bake for 1 hour.
Remove potatoes from the oven and let cool to room temperature.
Remove aluminum foil, peel and cut potatoes into 1¼-in. (3-cm) cubes,
and arrange in a large serving dish.
Slice the tomatoes, the eggs and the onions and scatter among
the potato cubes.
Place the sliced fish on top.
Mix olive oil, preserved lemon, lemon juice, salt, pepper and harissa
in a small bowl, then pour over the salad.
Leave at room temperature for 30 minutes to allow the flavors to merge.
Garnish with parsley and serve.

SHAKSHUKA WITH EGGPLANT

Tunisian Jewish immigrants brought shakshuka—a tomato and egg dish cooked in a frying pan—with them, and it soon became a distinct part of Israel's culinary personality. While new versions abound, featuring Merguez sausage, cheese, spinach, zucchini, or eggplant (as in this variation), the classic, spicy tomato shakshuka is still a definitive Israeli breakfast.

INGREDIENTS

2 medium eggplants
3 tbsp. olive oil
1 red onion, finely chopped
4 garlic cloves, minced
1 tbsp. finely chopped fresh
   green Anaheim chili, deseeded
2 cups (300 g) red cherry
   tomatoes, halved
1 tbsp. thyme
1 tsp. fine salt
1 tsp. freshly ground
   black pepper
4 large eggs

DIRECTIONS

Turn your oven to the grill setting and preheat to high.
Arrange whole eggplants in a roasting tray, prick them in two or three places with a fine knife to stop them from bursting, and roast until their skins are charred and they are soft to the touch.
Let cool to room temperature.
Heat olive oil in a large pan. Add onion, garlic, and chili, and fry until golden.
Add tomatoes and thyme and cook until tomatoes are very soft.
Continue cooking for 7 – 8 minutes, or until the sauce starts to thicken.
Meanwhile, peel the eggplants and cut the flesh into ¾-in.-wide (2-cm-wide) pieces.
Lower the heat, add half the salt and pepper to the pan, and stir well.
Carefully break the eggs directly into the pan, keeping some distance between them.
Place the pieces of eggplant between the eggs and season with the rest of the salt and pepper. Heat over low heat for 7 – 8 minutes until egg whites are set (the yolks should remain runny), then serve.

ISRAELI RATATOUILLE

A favorite among Mediterranean countries—especially France—ratatouille has always been a deceptively simple way to show off the flavors of the land, uniting vegetables that work separately but are oh so successful together. This colorful and joyful version is based on a variety of vegetables typical of Israeli and Middle Eastern cuisine.

INGREDIENTS

1 eggplant
1 red bell pepper
1 green bell pepper
1 large carrot, peeled
1 red onion
3 tbsp. olive oil
1 tbsp. coarse salt
½ tbsp. freshly ground
  black pepper

Sauce
3 tomatoes, coarsely grated
  with a box grater
1 tbsp. thyme leaves
1 clove garlic, minced
1 tsp. salt
½ tsp. finely chopped
  chili pepper
2 tbsp. olive oil

DIRECTIONS

Preheat oven to 430°F (220°C).
Cut eggplant, peppers, carrot, and onion into ⅓-in. (1-cm) cubes and place each vegetable in a separate small bowl.
Add 1 tbsp. of olive oil to the eggplant bowl. Add ½ tbsp. of olive oil to the other three bowls.
Season all four bowls with salt and pepper.
Line a roasting tray with baking paper.
Group the vegetables separately on the tray and roast until they are soft and golden (15–18 minutes for soft vegetables, 20–25 for hard ones).
Transfer roasted vegetables to a serving bowl.
In another bowl, combine all the sauce ingredients and mix well.
Pour sauce over the vegetables and serve.

FALAFEL

In Egypt, falafel is made with fava beans, while chickpeas are used in Greater Syria. They are often packed into pita and topped with salad and tahini, and Israelis even add sauerkraut, a strange but tasty twist from Eastern Europe. No matter how they are made, these small, fried balls are a beloved street food—as close as modern Israel gets to a national dish.

INGREDIENTS

2 cups (400 g) dried chickpeas
1 tsp. baking soda
4 garlic cloves
3 tbsp. breadcrumbs
½ cup (15 g) finely chopped
   fresh parsley
½ cup (15 g) coriander
1 tbsp. oregano
1 small onion, peeled and
   finely chopped
½ tsp. sweet paprika
½ tsp. ground cumin
1 tsp. salt
½ tsp. freshly ground
   black pepper
1 qt. (1 l) oil, for frying
Prepared tahini sauce,
   optional (page 290)

DIRECTIONS

Soak chickpeas overnight in a bowl with 2 qt. (2 l) of cold water and the baking soda.
Drain the chickpeas and put them back in the bowl.
Assemble a meat grinder with a small-hole plate.
Add the rest of the falafel ingredients to the chickpeas—except for the oil and tahini—then process the mix through the grinder.
Mix well again and refrigerate for 30 minutes.
Heat oil in a deep frying pan or large pot until very hot.
Make 25 ping-pong-ball-sized balls out of the mixture.
Moistening your hands with water helps.
Fry a few falafel balls at a time, until they rise to the surface and turn dark brown.
Using a slotted spoon, transfer falafel balls to a plate lined with paper towels to drain.
Serve warm, preferably with tahini sauce.

GOOD TO KNOW

While a meat grinder gets the best results, a food processor is also an option—just pulse carefully to avoid an overly soggy mixture.

DRIED BROAD BEANS, EGYPTIAN STYLE

You might have guessed from shakshuka that Israelis love their savory breakfast dishes. What might be dinner to many other cultures is the first meal of the day in this region. This savory bean stew is one of the Middle East's best-loved breakfast dishes. The hard-boiled egg gives it a hint of bright color as well as that familiar, comforting breakfast feel.

INGREDIENTS

1 lb. (500 g) dried brown
   broad beans
½ tsp. baking powder
4 hard-boiled eggs,
   whole and unpeeled

Seasoning
¼ cup (60 ml) extra virgin
   olive oil
4 garlic cloves, finely chopped
3 tbsp. freshly squeezed
   lemon juice
1 tsp. salt
½ tsp. freshly ground
   black pepper
½ tsp. ground cumin
1–2 tbsp. prepared tahini sauce,
   optional (page 290)

DIRECTIONS

Soak the broad beans overnight in 2 qt. (2 l) of cold water mixed with the baking powder.
The next morning, drain the beans, place them in a large saucepan, and add water to 1¼ in. (3 cm) above the beans.
Add the hard-boiled eggs and bring to a boil. Reduce the heat and simmer for 2 hours. The beans should be very soft, almost disintegrating. If necessary, cook for another 15 minutes.
Remove eggs from the pot, peel, and set aside.
Heat olive oil in a small saucepan. Add garlic and fry for a few seconds, until it begins to soften.
Turn the heat off and add the rest of the seasoning ingredients, except for the tahini, to the saucepan. Stir well and pour over the beans.
Mix the beans with the seasoning and transfer them to a serving dish. Quarter the eggs lengthwise and place on top.

GOOD TO KNOW

This dish is excellent when drizzled with tahini. Each region has a different way of making a tahini "dressing," but the easiest method is to mix it with lemon juice and olive oil until you achieve the desired consistency.

FISH AND SEAFOOD SOUP

Every Mediterranean country has at least one classic fish soup, and many have even more. Some, like the French bouillabaisse, have reached across borders to enchant hearts and fill stomachs all over the world. This common Israeli version, based on tomatoes, is light, gently seasoned, and may just become your new favorite.

INGREDIENTS

1 tbsp. olive oil

1 onion, finely chopped

2 garlic cloves, minced

1 pinch of saffron

1 tsp. fine salt

1 qt. (1l) fish stock (page 286)

½ cup (120 ml) tomato sauce (page 293)

7 oz. (200 g) calamari, cleaned and cut into rings

7 oz. (200 g) white fish fillet, cut into 1½-in. (4-cm) cubes

12 medium fresh shrimps, tails on

DIRECTIONS

Heat a wide saucepan, add olive oil, onion, and garlic, and sauté until lightly golden.

Add saffron and salt, and stir.

Add fish stock and tomato sauce, and stir.

Bring to a boil, then reduce the heat to low and simmer for 15 minutes.

Add the calamari and fish fillet, cook for 5 minutes, then add shrimp and cook for another 5 minutes.

Divide into 4 individual bowls and serve.

GRILLED SARDINES WITH HARISSA

Harissa, a red pepper-based condiment used in North African seasoning, has made a worldwide splash in the last decade. Used as a dried spice mixture or as a heady, sinus-clearing paste, it has appeared on menus from New York to London, flavoring stews, meats, and vegetarian dishes in unexpected ways. A touch of it goes a long way on this simple sardine dish.

INGREDIENTS

1⅓ lb. (600 g) small
   fresh sardines,
   3 – 3½ oz. (80 – 100 g) each
3 tbsp. harissa (page 293)
½ tsp. coarse salt
Juice of 1 lemon

DIRECTIONS

Arrange the sardines on a flat dish and brush with harissa on all sides.
Heat a heavy grilling pan over high heat.
Once the pan is blazing hot, carefully place the sardines on it.
Season with salt and grill until both sides are golden brown.
Transfer sardines to a serving dish, squeeze lemon juice on top, and serve.

STEAMED FISH FILLETS WITH YELLOW TOMATO SAUCE

Many varieties of tomato are grown in the greenhouses of Arava, then shipped to the coastal cities of Ashdod and Ashkelon, where Jews of North African descent incorporate them into a number of tasty dishes. This simple dish pairs white fish with the sweetness and acidity of fresh tomatoes, dialing up the bright color and flavor for which tomatoes are so prized.

INGREDIENTS

Sauce
3 tbsp. extra virgin olive oil, plus more for steaming fish
4 garlic cloves, minced
1 tbsp. finely chopped fresh green Anaheim chili, deseeded
3 cups (450 g) yellow cherry tomatoes
1 tsp. coarse salt

Fish
1⅓ lb. (600 g) fillets of white fish (like sole, halibut, sea bass, or red snapper), cut into 1¾ oz. (50 g) chunks
½ tsp. coarse sea salt
½ tsp. freshly ground black pepper
1 cup (40 g) fresh thyme leaves

DIRECTIONS

Heat olive oil in a medium saucepan. Add garlic and chili and fry until lightly golden.
Add tomatoes and salt and cook over medium heat, stirring, until the tomatoes release their juices. Reduce heat and simmer for 10 minutes.
Drain the tomatoes in a fine-mesh strainer placed over a bowl and use a wooden spoon to extract all their juices. Discard the tomato peels and seeds left in the strainer.
Transfer the tomato sauce to a small saucepan and cook over low heat until the sauce thickens.
Meanwhile, brush the fish with olive oil, season it with salt and pepper, and scatter the thyme leaves over the fillets.
Heat water in a large pot. Once it boils, put the fish fillets in a steamer basket and place the basket over the steaming water. Steam for 8 minutes.
Pour the warm sauce onto a serving plate, place the fish fillets on top, and serve.

GOOD TO KNOW

If you do not have a steamer basket, a fine mesh sieve with a sturdy base will work just as well.

DRIED FRUIT COUSCOUS

Sweet couscous, topped with dried fruit and seasoned with cinnamon, is a legacy of Morocco's Jews. While sweet couscous recipes are occasionally found in the Jewish communities of southern Morocco, for those in northern Morocco—a region near the Straits of Gibraltar once under Spanish rule—it is an all but essential component of their daily cuisine.

INGREDIENTS

1⅓ lb. (600 g) beef suitable
  for slow cooking,
  like shoulder or shank
2 tbsp. olive oil
1 onion, finely chopped
3 garlic cloves, minced
6 oz. (150 g) prunes, pitted
6 oz. (150 g) dried dates
6 oz. (150 g) dried apricots
2 tsp. salt
1 tsp. freshly ground
  black pepper
1 tsp. cinnamon
1½ qt. (1½ l) beef stock
  (page 289)
1 lb. (500 g) instant couscous,
  preferably Moroccan
½ cup (40 g) coarsely chopped
  toasted almonds

DIRECTIONS

Cut beef into cubes of about 1½ in. (4 cm) square.
Heat olive oil in a large saucepan over medium heat and sauté
the beef cubes on all sides.
Once they are evenly golden, transfer cubes to a bowl.
Add onion and garlic to the saucepan and sauté until lightly golden.
Return beef to the pot.
Add dried fruit, salt, pepper, cinnamon, and beef stock, and bring to a boil.
Reduce heat and simmer for 3 hours on the lowest heat.
If the broth is too thick, add half a cup of water.
Half an hour before the cooking time ends, place a perforated steamer
over the pan.
Add the couscous to the steamer. Cover and steam the grains for
the last 30 minutes.
Put the couscous in a bowl and mix well with a fork to break up any lumps.
Spread the couscous on a serving dish, pour the broth on top, garnish
with the toasted almonds, and serve.

ROASTED CHICKEN WITH GARLIC AND POTATOES

There is nothing quite as inviting as a whole roast chicken, straight out of the oven. This recipe uses lemon to its fullest advantage, first adding zest to the chicken before roasting, then blending it into the potato-based sauce. Even if you plan to serve the chicken in pieces, make sure to present it to the table first—you will want your guests to get the full impression.

INGREDIENTS

8 potatoes, cut lengthwise
   into 6 wedges each
8 garlic cloves, peeled
1 onion, cut into eighths
1 lemon, halved
1 large chicken
Extra virgin olive oil, for roasting
1 pinch coarse sea salt
1 pinch freshly ground
   black pepper

Sauce
1 large potato, washed
   and unpeeled
6 garlic cloves
2 tbsp. freshly squeezed
   lemon juice
½ tsp. lemon zest
1 tsp. sea salt
1 tsp. sweet paprika
½ cup (120 ml) extra virgin
   olive oil

DIRECTIONS

Preheat oven to 320°F (160°C).
Arrange potato wedges, garlic cloves, and onion sections on
a roasting tray, with the onions at the center.
Insert both lemon halves into the chicken's cavity, then place the chicken
on top of the onions in the tray.
Brush the chicken with some olive oil, season with salt and pepper,
and cover the tray with a double layer of aluminum foil.
Bake for 3 hours.
Meanwhile, wrap the large potato in aluminum foil and bake in the oven
for 90 minutes alongside the tray of chicken (and at the same temperature)
until soft.
Let the potato cool to room temperature, then slice lengthwise, peel,
and place in a food processor along with garlic, lemon juice, lemon zest,
salt, and paprika. While processing, trickle in the olive oil.
Process until texture resembles mayonnaise, then refrigerate.
After 3 hours of roasting, remove the aluminum foil from the chicken tray
and roast uncovered for another 20 minutes, until chicken is golden brown.
Let cool for 15 minutes, then serve with sauce on the side.

KEBAB SKEWERS

Kebab skewers are ubiquitous across the Middle East, Central Asia, and the Balkans. Each region has its own recipe— Israel alone has dozens of variations, from the Syrian Aleppo kebab to Iraqi, Romanian, and Turkish versions. Once you have got the essentials down, you can even start experimenting with your own versions—there is very little you can do wrong.

INGREDIENTS

1 lb. (500 g) ground veal
3½ oz. (100 g) ground lamb fat
2 tbsp. chopped parsley
1 onion, finely chopped
½ tbsp. cumin
½ tbsp. freshly ground
    black pepper
1 tbsp. coarse salt
¼ cup (60 ml) soda water

DIRECTIONS

Combine ingredients in a large bowl and knead by hand.
Mixture will be sticky at first but will quickly become smooth and elastic.
Stop kneading when the texture resembles that of soft dough,
and refrigerate for one hour.
Make 12 balls out of the mixture and prepare skewers with
one kebab ball on each.
Press and shape the balls into one 6-in.-long (15-cm-long) roll
and wind one around each skewer.
Heat a heavy frying pan or grill, and grill the skewers well on all sides.
Serve hot, preferably with a diced vegetable salad and some tahini
dressing (page 290).

SLOW-ROASTED BEEF SHOULDER WITH ONIONS

Oven-roasted cuts of beef are about as essential to Ashkenazi cuisine as chicken soup—full of flavor as well as comforting evocations of grandma's home cooking. This dish might look labor-intensive, but rest assured that most of its prep time is actually roasting time. With the meat safely in the oven, you are free to prepare other side dishes—and you should.

INGREDIENTS

2 tbsp. olive oil

5 garlic cloves, minced

2 tbsp. brown sugar

4 onions, cut into ⅓-in.-thick (1-cm-thick) slices

1 tsp. coarse salt

2 tsp. freshly ground black pepper

4½ lb. (2 kg) beef shoulder (preferably veal)

1 qt. (1 l) beef stock (page 289)

DIRECTIONS

Preheat oven to 355°F (180°C).

Heat olive oil in an oven-proof cast-iron pot.

Add garlic and brown sugar and cook until sugar has dissolved.

Add onions, salt, and pepper, and stir well.

Sweat the onions until they are soft and lightly golden.

Place beef shoulder on top of the onions and pour stock on top.

Bring to a boil, then remove from heat.

Cover the pot and roast in the oven for 1 hour.

Turn the beef over and roast it for another hour.

Using a large spoon or a ladle, baste the beef with the juices.

Cover the pot and continue roasting. Baste the beef 6 more times, once every 10 minutes, bringing the total roasting time to 3 hours.

Remove the pot from the oven and let cool for 40 minutes.

Carefully transfer beef to a cutting board. Using a sharp knife, cut into ⅕-in.-thick (½-cm-thick) slices.

Arrange slices in a deep serving dish. Heat beef juices in the pot and pour over beef slices.

Serve piping hot.

MARZIPAN-STUFFED DATES

A part of the dessert table presented during holidays and at special family occasions by Moroccan Jews, these tiny bites celebrate one of Israel's most successful exports—the humble but somehow decadent date, which grows all across the country. The simple flavor combination (dates, marzipan, walnut) somehow ends up being far more than the sum of its parts.

INGREDIENTS

Marzipan
9 oz. (250 g) blanched
    ground almonds
7 oz. (200 g) powdered sugar
3 drops almond extract
1 tsp. freshly squeezed
    lemon juice

20 Medjool dates,
    pitted and slit on one side
20 walnut halves

DIRECTIONS

Combine all the marzipan ingredients in a food processor and process for about 10 minutes, until the mixture is smooth with a texture like hard dough. Divide the mixture equally into 20 balls and shape each ball into a roll, roughly the length of a date.
Fill each date with a marzipan roll and top each with a walnut half.
Dates can be served immediately or kept for up to 3 days at room temperature in an airtight container.

SAND COOKIES

Jews of North African origin "imported" these sweet cookies to Israel. They have a crumbly texture and melt in the mouth, making them a great light dessert, snack, or accompaniment to tea or coffee. A few drops of rosewater or orange blossom extract make an interesting addition to the dough, and once out of the oven, the cookies can be sprinkled with fine brown muscovado sugar.

INGREDIENTS

7 oz. (200 g) unsalted cold butter
3½ oz. (100 g) cornstarch
4¼ oz. (120 g) flour
½ tsp. baking powder
½ tsp. salt
1¾ oz. (50 g) powdered sugar
2 tbsp. milk

DIRECTIONS

Combine the butter, cornstarch, flour, and baking powder in a food processor. Pulse only until crumbs form—take care not to let the dough come together into a ball yet.
Add the rest of the ingredients, then process just until a ball forms, taking care not to overprocess.
Remove the dough ball, wrap it with plastic wrap, and refrigerate for 30 minutes.
Preheat oven to 340°F (170°C).
Line a baking tray with baking paper.
Divide the dough equally into 20 balls and arrange on the tray, with 1¼ in. (3 cm) between them.
Bake for 20 minutes, until cookies are golden brown and a little cracked.
Let cool for 15 minutes before serving.
Cookies will keep well for up to 3 days in an airtight container.

FRUIT SALAD WITH LEMON VERBENA SYRUP

A fruit salad is all too often a consolation prize, a dessert by a chef who did not really want to make a dessert, or for guests who are too health-conscious to care. But the union of fresh, local, quintessential flavors in this colorful fruit salad makes it a fitting crown to any meal, and that unexpected note of lemon verbena is anything but ordinary.

INGREDIENTS

Syrup
½ cup (100 g) sugar
¼ cup (60 ml) water
1 tbsp. fresh lemon verbena leaves
½ tsp. lemon zest

Salad
7 oz. (200 g) strawberries
2 persimmons
2 oranges, segmented, membranes and seeds removed
Seeds of 1 pomegranate, stripped of skin and membranes
1 tsp. thyme leaves

DIRECTIONS

Combine all syrup ingredients in a small saucepan. Bring to a boil, stirring until the sugar dissolves.
Remove saucepan from heat and let it cool to room temperature.
Cut the strawberries and persimmons into $1/10$-in.-thick (3-mm-thick) slices and combine in a large serving bowl.
Add oranges, pomegranate seeds, and thyme leaves, then pour the syrup on top, mix gently, and serve.

SPICES, STOCKS, AND BUILDING BLOCKS

Whether you are a home cook or a professional chef, many if not most of your recipes will start with building blocks. These are the smaller prepared items, which chefs sometimes call mise en place, that all come together to make up a dish. Preparing them ahead of time will make the cooking experience quicker, more satisfying, and less hectic. Preparing them at home will definitely make for a better dish, offering more depth of flavor, not to mention a greater sense of pride in presenting a meal that was truly "made from scratch."

Middle Eastern dishes typically involve layers of texture and taste, and components of a dish often highlight not just one but several preparation techniques. Sweet, salty, sour, earthy, nutty, spicy—these aspects are mixed and matched to create complex, flavorful, and colorful dishes. But how do you know which flavors you are working with, how do you trust their freshness and intensity, unless you have made them yourself?

W hat follows is a selection of spice mixtures, stocks, sauces, and garnishes that are crucial to Middle Eastern cuisine. Use them exactly as called for in the recipes in this book or, once you have gotten comfortable with them, simply experiment. Slices of preserved lemon, for example, can be used to liven up the Acre-Style Vegetable Salad (page 38) and the Freekeh and Asparagus Salad (page 41), or add a sweet and sour pungency to any number of grilled meat or fish dishes in this book, like the Grilled Grouper with White Wine, Butternut Squash, and Olive Oil (page 66) or the Lamb Spare Ribs with Citrus Marinade (page 144).

Store-bought dry spice mixtures and pastes like harissa, za'atar, and baharat have improved in quality in recent years and become much easier to find, but there is nothing like a hand-labeled jar of homemade spice mix to complement a kitchen pantry, and nothing like a small pinch of it to enhance an already aromatic dish.

Tahini sauce makes a fitting topping or garnish for many a recipe in this book, and tomato sauce, of course, is the basis for the beloved dish shakshuka, as well as many other vegetable, meat, and fish dishes.

When it comes to adding depth of flavor to a dish, however, homemade stocks really do the trick. Page through the chapters of this book, and you will spot them as the base for soups, but also as a tasty foundation for slow-roasted leeks, boiled lentils, rice, and couscous, simmered fish stews, or even steamed dumplings.

Store-bought stocks have also become more sophisticated recently, but there is nothing like the deeply fragrant, gelatin-rich stock that comes from boiling bones, root vegetables, herbs, and spices for hours on end. Best of all, stocks are virtually free. Make them with leftover scraps from another meal (collect the remains of a roast chicken or grilled fish and just add water) or ask a butcher for the beef bones he would otherwise throw out. In addition, stocks are virtually everlasting. Freeze them in small, serving-size containers for later use. Or, even better, freeze tiny portions in ice cube trays for recipes that call for less than a cup—like the Seafood Pan Roast (page 138) or vegetable and grain dishes that just need a bit of enrichment.

Finally, if you are serious about bread, you have probably come across bakers who extol the virtues of making your own sourdough starter. Believe them. For anyone who is into the slow, satisfying process of mixing, kneading, proofing, and shaping, there are few miraculous kitchen moments to rival the experience of that first great, natural rise. Keeping a sourdough starter alive and well has been likened to nurturing a pet, and it is truly quite a responsibility. But it adds a complexity and richness to breads and bagels that cannot simply be bought.

Here, then, are the building blocks of Israeli and Palestinian cuisine. Go forth and make them.

When it comes to adding depth of flavor to a dish, however, homemade stocks really do the trick.

Previous page: **As delicious as it is, hummus can rarely stand alone.** Opposite page: **Once the chickpeas are boiled and mashed, you'll want to stir in plenty of tahini, and have a good thick bread to dip into the mix.**

VEGETABLE STOCK

INGREDIENTS

2 tbsp. extra virgin olive oil
2 carrots, chopped into
⅖-inch-thick (1-cm-thick) rounds
1 onion, finely chopped
3 garlic cloves, finely chopped
2 celery stalks, chopped into
⅖-inch-thick (1-cm-thick) slices
1 tbsp. thyme leaves
2 tbsp. finely chopped parsley
1 tbsp. coarse salt
1 qt. (1 l) water

DIRECTIONS

Heat olive oil in a wide saucepan. Add carrots, onion, garlic,
celery, thyme, and parsley and sauté over high heat until slightly softened.
Add salt and cook for another 2 minutes.
Add the water to the saucepan, bring to a boil, then reduce heat to low.
Simmer for 40 minutes, remove from heat, and strain stock.
Stock can be frozen in small airtight containers or in an ice cube tray
for small, easily portioned amounts.

FISH STOCK

INGREDIENTS

2 lb. (approx. 1 kg) bones from
fresh fish
1 thinly sliced carrot
1 leek, chopped
1 onion, chopped
3 sprigs of thyme
1 tsp. salt
1 tsp. chopped fresh green chili
1 head of garlic, halved
1 glass white wine
Half a lemon

DIRECTIONS

Place the fish bones in a large saucepan.
Add the vegetables, thyme, salt, chili, garlic, and white wine and bring
to a boil.
Add water to 1¼ in. (3 cm) above the vegetables.
Add the lemon half and return to a boil.
Reduce heat to low, and simmer gently for 1 hour.
Strain the stock, divide into small portions, and freeze.

BEEF STOCK

INGREDIENTS

1 lb. (500 g) beef bones
1 onion, chopped into 6 pieces
3 carrots, chopped into
⅘-in.-thick (2-cm-thick) slices
6 garlic cloves, coarsely crushed
1 leek, sliced into ⅘-in.-thick
(2-cm-thick) rings
2 cups (500 ml) red wine
10 sprigs of thyme
1 tbsp. coarse salt
2 qt. (2 l) water

DIRECTIONS

Preheat oven to 482°F (250°C).
Roast the bones, onion, carrots, garlic, and leek in a heavy,
oven-safe dish for 20 minutes, until golden-brown.
Remove dish from oven and place on the stove over high heat.
Add the wine, thyme, and salt and bring to a boil.
Cook for 4 minutes over high heat.
Add water and bring to a boil again.
Lower the heat, simmer for 2 hours, then strain.
Stock can be frozen in small airtight containers, or in an ice cube tray
for small, accessible amounts.

CHICKEN STOCK

INGREDIENTS

14 oz. (400 g) chicken bones
2 qt. (2 l) water
2 carrots, chopped into
⅖-in.-thick (1-cm-thick) slices
1 onion, peeled and quartered
2 celery stalks, chopped into
⅖-in.-thick (1-cm-thick) slices
1 tbsp. coarse salt

DIRECTIONS

Place all the ingredients in a large saucepan and bring to a boil
over high heat.
Lower the heat and simmer for 1 hour.
Strain the stock and allow it to cool.
Stock can be frozen in small airtight containers or in an ice cube tray
for small, easily portioned amounts.

TAHINI SAUCE

INGREDIENTS

1 cup (240 ml) raw tahini paste
Juice of ½ lemon
1 tsp. salt
1 cup (240 ml) cold water

DIRECTIONS

Whisk together tahini paste, lemon juice, salt, and ⅔ cup (160 ml)
cold water in a large bowl.
Add the rest of the water and mix well until the sauce is smooth and uniform.
If too thick or too runny, adjust the amount of water accordingly.

ZA'ATAR SPICE MIX

INGREDIENTS

4 tbsp. fresh za'atar (hyssop)
   or oregano leaves
1 tbsp. sumac
2 tbsp. white sesame seeds
½ tsp. salt

DIRECTIONS

Scatter the leaves on a baking sheet lined with baking paper
and place in an oven at 175°F (80°C) for 30 minutes.
Remove from the oven, chop the leaves very finely and mix well with
the other ingredients.
Store in a tightly sealed jar.

פפרקה
מעושנת
טנדורי
100/14
כורכום
סומק
SUMAK
100/14
קארי
גריל
עוף
ראס

BASIC TOMATO SAUCE

INGREDIENTS

3 tbsp. extra virgin olive oil
3 garlic cloves, minced
1 tsp. finely chopped
   fresh green chili pepper,
   deseeded
2 lb. (1 kg) assorted tomatoes,
   coarsely chopped, stems left on
   (It is worth mixing different
   varieties and colors of
   tomatoes, like Piccolo, Red
   Tiger, Green Tiger, and
   yellow tomatoes.)
1 tbsp. coarse salt

DIRECTIONS

Heat the olive oil in a wide saucepan. Add the garlic and chili pepper,
and fry until slightly golden.
Add the tomatoes and salt and cook over high heat, stirring occasionally.
Once the tomatoes' juices are released, turn down the heat and simmer
for 15 minutes, until tomatoes are soft.
Place a fine-mesh strainer over a large bowl.
Pour ⅓ of the sauce into the strainer and use a wooden spoon to press
the tomatoes well, extracting all the juices.
Discard tomato peel and seeds.
Repeat until all the sauce has been strained.
Sauce keeps well in the freezer for up to two weeks, in an airtight container.

HARISSA

INGREDIENTS

9 oz. (250 g) dried red peppers
2 garlic cloves
1 tsp. salt
1 tbsp. freshly squeezed
   lemon juice
½ cup (120 ml) olive oil

DIRECTIONS

Soak peppers in lukewarm water for 30 minutes, until soft.
Chop off their tops and remove the seeds.
Place the peppers, garlic, salt, and lemon juice in the bowl
of a standing mixer.
Run the mixer at medium speed and slowly pour in the olive oil.
Once a paste has formed, increase speed to maximum and carefully
pour in the rest of the oil.
Paste should be bright red, with an oily consistency.

SOURDOUGH STARTER

INGREDIENTS

Stage 1
1 tbsp. honey
3½ oz. (100 g) flour
3½ fl. oz. (100 ml) water

Stage 2
3½ oz. (100 g) flour
5⅓ oz. (150 ml) water

DIRECTIONS

In a bowl, mix all the stage 1 ingredients. Cover the bowl with
a dish towel and leave in a warm place. Allow the starter to ferment
at room temperature for 48–72 hours.
Add the stage 2 ingredients, mix well, and let the mixture rest for another
6–8 hours, until the mixture is fermented and full of bubbles.
At this stage, you can either repeat step 2 every day, pouring out about
half of the starter before adding the ingredients, until the starter has a
pungent aroma (approx. 1 week), or start experimenting with your starter.
You can also refrigerate it in an airtight container for several weeks.
When preparing it for use again, remove it from the refrigerator
and repeat stage 2 a day before use.

PRESERVED LEMONS

INGREDIENTS

6 lemons, cut widthways into
  1/10-inch-thick (5-mm-thick)
  slices
3 tbsp. coarse salt
1 tbsp. sweet paprika
¼ cup (60 ml) olive oil

DIRECTIONS

Arrange a layer of lemon slices at the bottom of a 2 qt. (2 l)
sanitized glass jar.
Sprinkle a little salt and paprika on top of the slices.
Repeat with the rest of the lemon slices.
Using another jar, push the lemon slices down into the jar, softening
them slightly and releasing their juices.
Pour the olive oil directly onto the lemon slices and around
the narrower jar.
Seal well, using plastic wrap or a lid, and leave in a dark place for a month.

Halal and Hamim, Malabi and Manakeesh, Ashkenazim vs. Sephardim. Are these delicious dishes, fresh ingredients, or cultural or religious terms to know? Consider this your cheat sheet.

AFIG
A pungent Bedouin spring cheese made of goat or sheep's milk left to dry in the sun and hot desert air.

ARAK
An anise-based drink served alongside many Middle Eastern dishes.

ASHKENAZIM
The Jews of Eastern Europe and the traditions and cuisines pertaining to them.

BALADI
An Arabic term meaning "local varieties."

BIBLICAL SEVEN SPECIES
Seven products mentioned in the Hebrew Bible that played and continue to play an important economic role in the region: wheat, barley, grapes, olives, figs, dates, and pomegranates.

BSISA
An ancient Bedouin "energy snack" with a sharp, smoky aroma made of toasted ground flour mixed with olive oil, water, sugar, and salt.

BULGUR
Durum wheat, a Middle Eastern grain staple, cooked as a side dish, mixed into salads, or ground to make flatbread.

CALZONES
A type of dumpling popular in Sephardic communities, brought to Israel by Spanish and Italian Jews.

CHALLAH
A yeasted, braided bread loaf traditionally eaten on Shabbat or Jewish holidays.

FALAFEL
Deep-fried balls of mashed chickpeas and spices, eaten on a platter or wrapped in a pita.

FREEKEH
Green roasted wheat, cooked much like couscous or bulgur, incorporated into salads or eaten as a side dish.

GEFILTE FISH
Stuffed, ground fish cakes traditionally eaten by Ashkenazi Jews on Shabbat or Jewish holidays.

HALAL
A term describing meat slaughtered under certain conditions pertaining to Muslim law.

HALVA
A crumbly paste made of sesame, often formed into cakes with other spices and served for dessert.

HAMIN
A slow-cooked stew or roast, meant to be left in the oven overnight, thereby circumventing the Jewish law against cooking food on the Sabbath.

HUMMUS
Ubiquitous Middle Eastern dish made out of mashed chickpeas, often blended with tahini.

KOFTA
A type of meatball found all over the Middle Eastern, Balkan, and Central Asian regions.

KOSHER
A term describing foods and preparation methods that adhere to a strict set of Jewish dietary laws.

KREPLACH
A Yiddish word for small, boiled dumplings with a number of fillings, usually served in soup.

KUBBEH
Stuffed bulgur or semolina dumplings found throughout the Middle East.

KUGEL
A slow-cooked noodle or potato dish, usually eaten by Ashkenazi Jews on Shabbat.

LABANEH
A type of strained, white cheese prominent in Israeli and Palestinian cooking.

LUBIYA
A name for both black-eyed peas and the stew made from them.

MAAMOUL
Sweet, flaky shortbread cookies filled with a variety of fruits and nuts, with origins in Levantine cuisine and close ties to the Muslim festival of Eid, marking the end of Ramadan.

MALABI
A type of cream-based custard dessert popular in the Middle East, originating in the Arabic cuisine of the Middle Ages.

MANAKEESH
An olive-oil-rich flatbread baked with a variety of toppings.

MAQLUBA
An "upside-down" rice and meat casserole; a staple of Palestinian cuisine.

MASAKHAN
An Arab and Palestinian staple served during the olive harvest; chicken roasted with olive oil and spices and served on top of pita bread.

MATFUNA
The Arabic word for "buried" as well as the name of a Bedouin preparation method that involves slow-cooking whole animals by burying them in a pit lined with glowing embers.

MEZE
Little shared plates of cold and warm dishes.

SABRA
The fruits of the prickly pear bush; also a slang term for Jews who were born in Israel.

SAYADIEH
A classic fisherman's dish of seafood and rice, meant to make the most of cheap fish.

SHAKSHUKA
A beloved dish in Israel, made from eggs cooked in a rich tomato sauce, and sometimes other vegetables.

SHAMI CUISINE
The cuisine of Greater Syria.

SHAWARMA
A popular Turkish and Arabic street food dish made of sliced meat wrapped in a pita with salads and sauces.

SENIYEH
A low, round dish used for cooking, baking, and serving; also the name of the type of stew cooked in one.

SEPHARDIM
The Jews of Spain, North Africa, Iraq, Turkey, and the Balkans and the dishes and cuisines pertaining to them.

SOFRITO
A type of Sephardic roast popular across the Mediterranean.

SUMAC
A type of spice made from the ground, deep red berries of the sumac bush; a component of the za'atar spice mixture.

TABUN
A type of clay oven used by generations of Palestinians to cook breads, stews, and meat dishes.

TAHINI
A sauce made from toasted, ground sesame seeds, often mixed into hummus or used as a topping for a variety of dishes.

ZA'ATAR
A spice mixture traditionally made from ground, dried hyssop leaves, toasted sesame seeds, sumac, and salt.

DIVINE FOOD

Israeli and Palestinian Food Culture and Recipes

David Haliva would like to thank
Keren Rattenbach, Keren Friedland,
Hadar Makov, David Laxer,
Aviram Mazayov, and Elianna Bar-El.

Edited by **David Haliva, Sven Ehmann,** and **Robert Klanten**

Research and writing: **Ronit Vered**
Translation from Hebrew: **Tali Kord**
Text editing: **Diana Rubanenko** and **Kevin Brochet**
Additional text, editing, and research: **Giulia Pines**

Chef: **Avner Laskin**
Sous chef: **Adam Mizrachi**
Food styling: **Nurit Kariv**

Photography: **Dan Perez**
Photographic assistance: **Nicky Trok**

Layout and cover: **Ludwig Wendt, Léon Giogoli,** and **David Haliva**
Creative direction design: **Ludwig Wendt** and **David Haliva**
Cover photography: **Dan Perez**
Typefaces: **Avenir** by **Adrian Frutiger** and **Adobe Garamond Pro**
by **Claude Garamond** and **Robert Slimbach**
Additional images by **Sivan Askayo** (pp. 5, 6, 8 top, 56, back cover bottom right),
Sean Pavone/Shutterstock (p. 160), **Posztos/Shutterstock** (p. 291),
Amarita/Shutterstock (p. 97 top right), and **Protasov AN/Shutterstock** (p. 87)

Editorial management: **Adam Jackman** and **Silvena Ivanova**
Proofreading: **Bettina Klein**

Printed by **Nino Druck GmbH, Neustadt/Weinstraße**
Made in Germany

Published by **Gestalten, Berlin 2016**
ISBN 978-3-89955-642-1

German edition, ISBN 978-3-89955-666-7

Bibliographic information published by the Deutsche Nationalbibliothek.
The Deutsche Nationalbibliothek lists this publication in the Deutsche Nationalbibliografie;
detailed bibliographic data are available online at http://dnb.d-nb.de.

This book was printed on paper certified according to the standards of the FSC®.

MIX
Paper from
responsible sources
FSC® C006655